A History of Tri-ang and Lines Brothers Ltd

A History of Tri-ang and Lines Brothers Ltd
The Rise and Fall of the World's Largest Toy-Making Company

Kenneth D. Brown

PEN & SWORD HISTORY
AN IMPRINT OF PEN & SWORD BOOKS LTD.
YORKSHIRE - PHILADELPHIA

First published in Great Britain in 2022 by
Pen & Sword History
An imprint of
Pen & Sword Books Ltd
Yorkshire – Philadelphia

Copyright © Kenneth D Brown 2022
ISBN 978 1 52679 317 1

The right of Kenneth D Brown to be identified as Author of this work has been asserted by him in accordance with the Copyright, Designs and Patents Act 1988.

The Author has taken reasonable steps to trace the copyright holder to obtain permission for use of images but, despite his best endeavours, has been unable to do so. The copyright holder, or the late copyright holder's estate, is advised to make themselves known to the Publishers.

A CIP catalogue record for this book is
available from the British Library.

All rights reserved. No part of this book may be reproduced or transmitted in any form or by any means, electronic or mechanical including photocopying, recording or by any information storage and retrieval system, without permission from the Publisher in writing.

Typeset in 11.5/14 Ehrhardt by Vman Infotech Pvt. Ltd.

Printed and bound by CPI Group (UK) Ltd, Croydon, CR0 4YY

Pen & Sword Books Limited incorporates the imprints of Atlas, Archaeology, Aviation, Discovery, Family History, Fiction, History, Maritime, Military, Military Classics, Politics, Select, Transport, True Crime, Air World, Frontline Publishing, Leo Cooper, Remember When, Seaforth Publishing, The Praetorian Press, Wharncliffe Local History, Wharncliffe Transport, Wharncliffe True Crime and White Owl.

For a complete list of Pen & Sword titles please contact

PEN & SWORD BOOKS LIMITED
47 Church Street, Barnsley, South Yorkshire, S70 2AS, England
E-mail: enquiries@pen-and-sword.co.uk
Website: www.pen-and-sword.co.uk

Or
PEN AND SWORD BOOKS
1950 Lawrence Rd, Havertown, PA 19083, USA
E-mail: Uspen-and-sword@casematepublishers.com
Website: www.penandswordbooks.com

Acknowledgements

In writing this book I have benefitted in numerous ways from the generosity of others. I am particularly grateful to Anthony Lowth for granting permission to reproduce several images from his edition of Peggy Lines' privately printed history of the Lines family businesses, to Peter van Lune for allowing me to use photographs from his definitive history of FROG and Penguin models, to Essential Works for permitting me to reproduce a digitised picture from *Hornby: The Official Illustrated History*, to Wallis and Wallis Auctioneers for pictures of Tri-ang dolls' houses, and to Jon Mountfort for permission to reprint an illustration from his book, *Scalextric Collectibles*. My efforts to contact copyright holders of a few other pictures used in this book received no response. If you own copyright to these, or know who does, please contact the publisher. Gary Haines kindly facilitated my access to the uncatalogued Peggy Lines papers at the Museum of Childhood, while Roddy Young and Chris Morris each drew my attention to detailed aspects of Lines' history which I might otherwise have overlooked. Andrew and Laura Brown provided sterling assistance, respectively in preparing the text and the illustrations. Special thanks are due also to my friend and sometime colleague at Queen's University, John Wilson, whose detailed comments and insights greatly improved the finished product, and to Lester Crook who encouraged me to write this book.

Contents

Acknowledgements		v
Chapter One	Learners: Fathers and Sons, 1850–1918	1
Chapter Two	Going Solo, 1918–1929	28
Chapter Three	Rough Roads, 1929–1945	54
Chapter Four	The Highway, 1945–1961	83
Chapter Five	The Wheels Come off, 1961–1971	109
Chapter Six	In the Breaker's Yard	142
Notes		155
Bibliography		173
Index		177

List of Tables

Table 1	Statement Showing Progress of Lines Brothers from Commencement	37
Table 2	Lines Brothers Ltd. Turnover and Profit 1925–1929	48
Table 3	Lines Brothers Ltd. Annual Pre-tax Profit 1930–1940	56
Table 4	Hamley Brothers. Costs as a Percentage of Sales	60
Table 5	Lines Brothers Ltd. Issued Capital 1920–1935	77
Table 6	Lines Brothers Ltd. Profit 1940–1945	82
Table 7	Lines Brothers Ltd. Financial Performance 1952–1961	106
Table 8	Lines Brothers Ltd. Results for Year Ending 31 December 1961–1970	112
Table 9	Total Toy Imports to the UK 1960–1968	122
Table 10	Lines Brothers Ltd. Ratio of Non-productive to Productive Wages 1967–1968	148

Chapter One

Learners: Fathers and Sons, 1850–1918

In 1806 a glass trinket maker, Thomas Osler, travelled from his Birmingham home to London for the first time in his life. Whilst in the capital he was offered a contract to supply £500 worth (the equivalent in today's terms of £46,000) of glass eyes for dolls. He did not identify the potential contractor but it was probably one of the highly skilled European doll makers, perhaps even a member of the Montarini or Pierotti families who had settled in the capital to pursue their craft. Nor did Osler take on the work, but he later calculated that if every girl in Britain between the ages of 2 and 7 were to receive a new doll annually, then the trade in dolls' eyes alone would be worth many thousands of pounds. Given prevailing levels of child mortality and poverty, his underlying premise was highly dubious: dolls with glass eyes were expensive and generally only accessible to the relatively well off. Furthermore, his observation may have seemed somewhat trite at a time when Britain had just emerged from a quarter of a century's conflict with France which had ended on the bloodied fields of Waterloo. But as he told a parliamentary select committee in 1824, his calculation was intended to show precisely 'the importance of trifles'.[1] Fifty years later these trifles had assumed a greater importance, as George Bartley, a civil servant and later Tory MP, observed:

> Accustomed to fix our attention on those articles, whose use is principally confined to persons of adult age, whether by adding to their comfort, or for their necessary daily requirements ... we are apt to lose sight of the fact that children too have their wants, which are only to be supplied by those little trifles that we call Toys, and to ignore the extent to which their manufacture in Britain is carried on.[2]

By the time Bartley wrote this, Britain's employment, output, and trade were dominated by mining, shipbuilding, textiles, engineering and iron – the industries which lay at the heart of the industrial revolution and which, by mid-century, had transformed the nation into the world's workshop. The site map of manufacturing activity published alongside the 1851 national census was dark with dense clusters of tiny icons representing the main locations of these huge industries. Yet those who took time to study the map more carefully would have also spotted a couple of wheeled horses, symbols of an indigenous toy industry whose quiet development over the previous decades had been pretty well obscured by the belching smoke of the factory chimneys and railway locomotives, the roar of the spinning and weaving machines, the hammerings of the shipbuilders and engineers, and the growing heaps of mine waste despoiling parts of the countryside. Yet as Bartley suggested, the vast wealth generated by Britain's economic progress was also creating a demand for newer, consumer-based manufactures, the more so as prosperity gradually percolated down through the social orders and generations. Children were among the main beneficiaries.

Historically, the children of the wealthy had always had access to commercially or professionally made playthings. Doubtless it was they who received the German dolls being imported through Southampton in the early sixteenth century, or the puppets and balls against which Thomas South railed so vigorously.[3] For the majority, however, such playtime as a brief childhood allowed was generally served by what nature provided or what a handy parent might occasionally be able to cobble together. But by the mid-eighteenth century the demand for commercially manufactured toys was spreading to the middling classes, especially in London where William Hamley established his toy shop in 1760. By 1822, the capital's inhabitants were sufficiently numerous and prosperous to support eighty-four toy retailers and wholesalers, while a similar trend was evident in the provinces, with Norwich, Manchester and York all boasting toy dealers by the 1820s where none had existed in the 1780s.[4] Jane Austen took it for granted that in rural Wiltshire Caroline Morland, the heroine of her 1803 novel *Northanger Abbey* and the daughter of a comfortably off clergyman, should have played with dolls.⁵ So widespread was the availability of toys by this time that when Maria Edgeworth and her father were preparing their well-known 1812 treatise on children's education, they considered including 'an inventory of the present most fashionable items in our toy shops'.⁶ However, that was a task more easily imagined than undertaken, if only because not all toy shops and dealers were handling children's playthings exclusively, or even at all. It is true that as early as 1800 London already possessed a couple of shops specialising in rocking horses, but contemporaries generally were still using the word 'toy' very broadly, applying it as well to a whole variety of miniatures and small items intended for adult use – buckles, brooches, knick-knacks and so on. It was not really until the 1880s that such artefacts were more commonly described as 'fancy goods' and for much of the century, therefore, the distinction between adults' and children's toys remained blurred. Thus in her 1862 novel, *Lady Audley's Secret*, Mary Braddon referred variously to a watch, a purse, and small ornaments as well as a blue-eyed wax doll as the sort of items 'to be found in a toy-shop'.⁷ Nevertheless, there was a discernible shift towards specialisation in children's playthings, especially in London where the number of toy shops grew to more than 270 by 1830.⁸ They were particularly concentrated in the Burlington and Lowther arcades where, according to *Punch*, unwary shoppers ran the risk of putting their feet through drums or falling over trays full of children's tea things.⁹

The Edgeworths' work reflected a developing contemporary interest, not only in education broadly defined but also, more specifically, in the notion of toys as instruments of socialisation and instruction. Rising real incomes and statutory restrictions on child labour also worked to boost the domestic demand for children's toys. Much of it was satisfied by European makers benefitting from successive reductions in import tariffs, which were abolished altogether in 1853. Although the absolute accuracy of the trade figures is questionable, the declared value of toy imports to Britain rose from just under £6,000 in 1820 to almost £50,000 in 1855. By the time Bartley wrote, the figure had rocketed to £393,000.¹⁰ Yet as early as 1835 the economist J. R. McCulloch was stressing that toys, which he took care to define as 'trifling article(s) made expressly for the amusement of children', had 'in late years . . . been made in greater abundance in England than formerly'.[11] That, too, was a claim reiterated by Bartley in the 1870s, and apparently vindicated by the occupational statistics contained in the decennial censuses which showed an increase in those describing themselves as toy makers from 1,139 in 1831 to 2,502 by 1871.

The trend is clear even if the figures cannot be regarded as reliable and are almost certainly too low. For one thing, the enumerators tended to classify as unoccupied anyone who was currently out of work – and in toy making both unemployment and underemployment were rife. Many of those who spoke to Henry Mayhew when he investigated the trade for the *Morning Chronicle* in 1850 commented on the volatile nature of demand and its vulnerability to the seasons, the weather, general economic conditions and fashionable whim. 'When the labouring people are out of employ,' one interviewee told him, 'I feel it in my business.'[12] Even war affected demand, with Mayhew noting that the ending of the conflict with Napoleon had greatly reduced the appeal of martial toys such as guns and drums.[13] The move to free trade which characterised British commercial policy in the post-Napoleonic years worked in the same direction, one aggrieved soft toy maker complaining bitterly that 'the introduction of French and foreign toys at the reduced rate of duty has affected me a wonderful sight. This lamb can't be made in London for a penny, but it's bought from Germany and sold here retail at a penny.'[14] A tin toy maker had been similarly undercut, pointing out that 'foreigners have got all the trumpet trade now – what we got 30s a gross for we only get 7s now.'[15]

A further problem with the occupational figures in the censuses arose because job definitions were often rather vague, changing over time, and certainly unable to accommodate either the reality that individuals often drifted in and out of particular trades or that in some manufacturing enterprises, output could be both for children and adults. This is very apparent, for example, from the records of the Sun Fire Office whose insured clients in the early years of the nineteenth century included numerous individuals such as John Bell of Covent Garden, listed as a 'toy and pianoforte maker'.[16] Such overlaps explain why the *Business Directory of London,* published in 1864, included pewterers as well as manufacturers of drums, tambourines, dominoes, India rubber, tin ware and kites among its forty-six listed toy makers, while simultaneously advising readers in search of children's toys to look under headings as diverse as balls, backgammon boards, dolls, fishing rods, magic lanterns, puzzles and rocking horses.[17] Almost certainly therefore, many of those making playthings for children, perhaps as a sideline or on a seasonal basis, were not categorised as such in the censuses. This was particularly likely in the case of woodworkers whose skills could easily be turned to toys. Adding those classified as woodworkers, makers of bats and balls, masks, fishing rods, and modellers in various materials to the official 1871 figure for toy makers takes the total to 3,753. That year's census was probably the most accurate and comprehensive to date, but even this recalculated figure is probably on the low side: it is certainly well below the 22,800 toy makers and wood carvers suggested a few years before by the statistician Leone Levi.[18] Levi's estimate was inflated by the inclusion of Warwickshire toymen whose main output consisted of toys in the broader, traditional sense, but it was the case that several of the midland makers did cater for children, in particular turning out glass eyes for dolls and penny tin toys.

Finally, it is clear that the early censuses in particular probably omitted altogether some of those engaged in making toys for children. The 1831 exercise, for instance, gathered information pertaining only to males aged over 20, thus missing out the many women who, as their inclusion in the 1851 count revealed, constituted by then over a third of those engaged in the trade. Many children were also to be found in the business and Charles Dickens got it right when he gave his fictional toy maker Caleb Plummer a daughter to assist him in his work.[19] Mayhew certainly encountered several toymen whose only other labour input came from their wives and children, or whose employees were juveniles. This was characteristic of small enterprises where narrow profit margins and fluctuating demand made low labour costs imperative. Fairly typical, therefore, was the maker of Bristol toys (small, usually wheeled, wooden playthings) interviewed by Mayhew. He employed 'two boys . . . one was an apprentice, a well-grown lad: the other was a little fellow who had run away from a city institution.'[20]

Most of those interviewed by Mayhew worked at the lower end of the market, scraping a tenuous and uncertain living from their cramped homes clustered predominantly in the Clerkenwell and Aldgate districts of London. Some were in effect middle men, albeit poor ones, making parts for others to assemble. Mayhew noted the prevalence of this arrangement with respect to sewed dolls, for example. He met one individual who made composition heads which were then taken away to be painted, fitted with glass eyes from Birmingham and then dressed by female knitters working on a putting-out basis. It was, he noted, a precarious business, and the man's weekly earnings of about twelve shillings (sixty pence) left him 'in grinding poverty. His cheeks were sunk . . . like a man half dead.'[21] Equally badly off were the self-employed garret masters, described by the commissioners to the 1851 Great Exhibition as seldom manufacturing to order but making a few items and then hawking them around the streets and shops. 'Without capital and compelled to work, almost literally from hand to mouth, they continue to exist only, without any material advance . . . making the same kinds . . . one year after another.'[22] Such makers depended heavily on impulse buying and were particularly vulnerable to trade depressions, one dealer telling Mayhew that they often starved because they were constantly undercutting each other's prices.[23] Those turning out small wooden toys also had to compete against similar items imported from Germany, parts of which were so densely forested that in 1871 an entire pine trunk could be purchased for as little as 2d (less than 1p). Things were not much better for small-scale manufacturers of metal and mechanical toys, sectors dominated respectively by the Germans and the French. Nuremburg's emergence as a centre of metal goods production from the fifteenth century had given it a head start in terms of manufacturing efficiency and establishing distribution networks, while smaller English makers simply lacked the skills to make decent mechanical toys, one retailer telling Mayhew that he doubted the capacity of British workers even to repair broken French toys.[24]

But not all of the growing number of toy makers in Britain were so badly placed, and even in the 1850s Mayhew found a few who made a good living, producing high-quality goods for the wealthy end of the market. There was, for example, the French immigrant who employed eight women in his workshop to produce hair-covered papier-mâché animals selling for as much as £5 each, and the manufacturer of toy theatres who claimed that at the height of their popularity in the 1840s he had made £30 a week, and the individual based in High Holborn who turned out talking dolls for six guineas (£6.30) each.[25] Then there was William B. Britain who moved from Birmingham to London in 1845 and, eventually with the assistance of his numerous children, earned a reasonable income by making simple mechanical toys in his home-based workshop in Hornsey. (Later his eldest son, also William, would invent a way of casting the hollow lead soldiers with which the family name became synonymous.) Makers of the better-quality items often produced to order for wholesalers or retailers. Such was Dickens's Caleb Plummer, whose output for the merchants Gruff and Tackleton included dolls, Noah's arks, little carts, fiddles, drums, cannons, shields, swords, boats and 'dozens upon dozens of grotesque figures'.[26] To these may be added the makers of large wooden toys which were too expensive for the Europeans to export, and which by the middle of the century were already widely recognised as something of a British speciality: so much so that the official report commented with some surprise on their absence from the Great Exhibition of 1851, noting that 'none of the ordinary strong toys of English manufacture are contributed.'[27] What they had in mind were the rocking horses, wheeled carts, and dolls' houses of the sort owned by the children's writer E. E. Nesbit during her 1860s childhood and produced by well-established and relatively large-scale enterprises such as J. & T. Thorp of Manchester, J. E. Ridingbery, originally a Bristol-based spinning top maker, the Collinson Brothers whose factory in Liverpool was visited by Queen Victoria in 1851, and F. H. Ayres, son of a cabinet maker who also became a leading manufacturer of rocking horses.[28] Probably the best-known business of all at mid-century, however, was that run by William Henry Cremer, son of a wood carver from Germany. Like his fictional counterparts Gruff and Tackleton, Cremer bought in from small makers to supply his two London retail outlets, but he also had his own manufacturing premises producing wheeled carts, rocking horses, dolls and other quality items. His substantial advertisement in *Peter Parley's Annual* for 1863 indicated that he was catering mainly for the top end of the market, for in it he claimed to be a manufacturer and importer of toys not only for the British royal family but also for the royal houses of Prussia, France and Austria. This seems credible, given that he was the only British toy maker to exhibit at the Paris international exhibition in 1867.[29] Not long afterwards he wrote a short book taking issue with the widespread perception that the English 'don't profess to do much in this line' and arguing that British-made toys were 'coveted in every nursery'. Nor, as he went on to point out, was it merely a matter of wooden toys, for 'we excel in other branches', in particular moveable wax dolls, mechanical novelties, drums and educational toys.[30] Such testimony from one so prominent in the trade provides powerful support for Bartley's claim, three years later, that 'the manufacture of toys has long since ceased to be carried on exclusively on a small scale . . . a considerable amount of intelligence, capital, and skill have been brought to bear on this industry.'[31]

Even as Bartley was putting pen to paper, two brothers, George and Joseph Lines, were about to bring their intelligence, capital and skills to the industry. From the early 1860s George Lines, a wood carver, had been making wooden horses by hand in a small factory in London's East End. In 1866 he moved to new premises in Kings Cross Road. There he was joined by his younger brother, Joseph, who, despite his classification in the census as a rocking horse maker, had taken on several unrelated jobs, most recently in a local branch of the Co-operative Wholesale Society. Shortly afterwards, they formally registered their business partnership as G. & J. Lines (hereafter referred to as G. & J.) and moved to a new site at 457 Caledonian Road. Whether these were calculated decisions or merely fortuitous ones, the timing could not have been better since the new structure and superior premises put them in an ideal position to benefit from the almost exponential increase in the demand for toys which developed in Britain over the following decades. In part, this was a simple matter of demographics. Deaths among those under 15 fell by almost a quarter between 1850 and 1900. Given that the population was growing anyway, the result was that the 7,300,000 children of 1850 had become 10,500,000 by 1900. Over the same period a reduction in average family size, noticeable first among the middle classes and then extending into the artisanate, meant that average per capita income within individual families was higher. On top of that, falling food prices pushed up real wages by some seventy-five per cent over the last three decades of the nineteenth century, and if that rate of increase slowed somewhat during the Edwardian years, real wages still remained higher than they had been, even in the 1880s. The net outcome was an increase in per capita income of some forty-four per cent between 1870 and 1910.[32]

The evidence of this growing affluence was everywhere – more holidays, more professional sport and recreational hobbies, the heyday of the music hall, the acquisition of household furnishings, the burgeoning popular press and the rapid development of new light consumer industries, including toys.[33] Averages, of course, merely summarise extremes, and as the social surveyors scurrying around the tail end of the century emphasised, it remained the case that for the offspring of that third of the urban population still in relative poverty, commercially made playthings remained pretty much out of reach. In the 1860s, John Hollingshead had described Whitechapel children playing with oyster shells and broken crockery.[34] Things were apparently little changed half a century later when Maud Pember Reeves noted the absence of either books or games in the homes of Lambeth children.[35] Seebohm Rowntree confirmed that poor city children could expect no money for dolls, marbles or sweets, while in rural areas low levels of disposable income effectively ruled out the purchase of 'toys and dolls and picture books, even of the cheapest quality'.[36] Yet even for children such as these, the occasional toy might be channelled their way via an altruistic individual, a philanthropic institution, or a church desirous of bolstering Sunday School attendance. Children living on the Corsham estates of Sir John Poynder, for example, regularly received from the landlord a Christmas toy.[37] From 1879, the journal *Truth*, founded by the radical politician Henry Labouchère and which at one time had a circulation of over a million, organised an annual exhibition of toys which were then distributed to institutions catering for the children of the poor – hospitals, infirmaries, workhouses, and poor law schools. The event, held in London's Albert Hall and which ceased only with the outbreak of war in 1914, was deemed to be of sufficient importance to merit a regular report in the columns of *The Times*.

But this expansion of Britain's domestic toy market was not merely a matter of charitable impulse, numbers and disposable incomes. Legislation also played a part. Following the passage of the Ten Hours Act in 1847, successive reductions in the time children were legally allowed to work gradually allowed a more clear-cut distinction to emerge between adulthood and childhood, reinforcing the notion that children were not merely smaller inhabitants of the world of work – which historically they had shared with adults – but rather a distinctive group of beings with its own identity and specific needs. By the 1890s, only about a third of boys and a fifth of girls between the ages of 10 and 14 were still gainfully employed, the implication being that working-class children in particular had more free time.[38] If ultimately that was reduced by the introduction first of compulsory (1872) and then of free (1883) education, these measures in themselves further reinforced the distinction between children (school) and adults (work), resulting in a more uniform length of childhood across the nation and underlining the educational significance of toys, long-acknowledged but now increasingly so. Toys may have been regarded as trifles, proclaimed *The Graphic* in 1871, but 'to children these trifles are a real matter of education as well as of pleasure'.[39] In similar vein, Bartley also argued that it was misleading to dismiss 'objects which we all require to use during a great part of our early life, and *which have such an immense influence on us*, and add so much to the happiness of our earliest years.'[40] Likewise, when the Sociological Society organised an exhibition of toys in 1908, it was with the intent of allowing philanthropists, sociologists and educators to throw 'more light on the character, predilections and latent possibilities of the young'.[41] Not surprisingly, perhaps, the *Fancy Goods and Toy Trades Journal* commented in 1891 that 'in the progress made in toys and games for children it is noticeable that those which have a distinctly educational purpose . . . are increasing relatively in numbers and apparently in popularity.'[42]

The very existence of this publication, and indeed of several others catering specifically for all those engaged in the toy business, was in itself further testimony to the rapid development of an indigenous industry in the last decades of the nineteenth century. So, too, was the substantial increase and growing geographical dispersion of toy dealers as evidenced in an analysis of trade directories. In the thirty years or so prior to 1900, the number in Leeds doubled: in Manchester it more than doubled and in Newcastle it tripled.[43] Many of these were merchants handling the imported toys which certainly went some way towards satisfying growing British demand, albeit to nothing like the extent claimed by E. E. Williams, a near-hysterical and politically motivated propagandist whose misguided writings helped spawn the enduring myth that the nurseries of Victorian Britain were effectively Teutonic colonies.[44] It is true that the value of German-originated toys entering Britain rose to almost £800,000 in 1900, but this has to be set into context. As the world's wealthiest and premier trading nation, it was almost inevitable that Britain should receive the largest share of the increased exports resulting from the massive expansion of global commerce which occurred between 1870 and 1914. What Williams failed to mention, however, was that the German *proportion* of Britain's toy imports remained fairly stable at about three-quarters. In other words, while more German toys were certainly being sold in Britain, they by no means swamped other foreign toys or, more importantly, inhibited the growth of the indigenous manufacturing sector. Indeed, rising prosperity was generating such a widespread demand that, even as Williams was prophesying doom and gloom, British entrepreneurs were establishing many of the firms whose products would increasingly fill the nation's toy cupboards or, in the case of William Harbutt's plasticine, burrow its way into the nation's carpets. Prominent among them were Roberts Brothers and Chad Valley, best known for their boxed games, the rag book makers, Dean's, Farnell and Chiltern in soft toys, Bassett-Lowke with its intricately engineered model locomotives, Britain's hollow cast lead soldiers, and Frank Hornby's Mechanics Made Easy, very quickly rebranded as Meccano. With so many new enterprises, it was not surprising that the occupational census identified almost 7,000 individuals working in the trade by 1891. Even that was still an underestimate because it overlooked the small garret masters and individuals working on their own account.

The latter included a youthful Charlie Chaplin who was driven to find a more lucrative outlet for his talents when his mother complained that her blouses were being ruined by his use of the family laundry bucket to boil up the glue which he needed for the penny boats he was then making and selling.

This then was the highly favourable background against which George and Joseph Lines were able to develop their new business venture. With a floor area of some 25,000 square feet, the Caledonian Road factory provided adequate space for the significant number of employees required to make goods that, for the most part, still involved a considerable amount of skilled hand work. Expansion was rapid; a surviving photograph showed that by 1891 there were some forty individuals in the steam works alone, while the total workforce of about 150 made it, so it was later claimed, the largest toy concern in the country.[45] Their employers were hard taskmasters. George, whose primary responsibility was oversight of the actual manufacturing, discouraged the singing of certain songs in the paint shop on the grounds that it slowed down the men's work rate. Joseph took charge of the sales and office work, including the disbursement of the men's wages, a role which revealed his martinet tendencies since he proved habitually suspicious of any individual whose weekly earnings exceeded thirty shillings (£1.50). Their toughness was obviously effective, however, for an extraordinary range of toys trundled from the works – painted engines, trucks, brewers' drays, tramcars, swings, carts, pole horses, nursery yachts, wheelbarrows, wheeled horses, and rocking horses. It was an array of precisely the sort of heavy wooden toys in which British makers had always enjoyed some comparative advantage over continental rivals. Small wonder that a contemporary trade paper should comment in 1896 that in the class of products made by Lines, 'neither the Germans nor the Americans can beat us'.[46]

By the time this was written, the next generation of Lines boys, as was common in Victorian Britain, was ready to follow their fathers into the family business. The eldest of Joseph's sons, Will, was initially apprenticed to an office but in 1896 he went into the factory, along with his younger brother Walter, who was then 14 years old. If they expected favours they were disappointed. In a working week of five days, each twelve hours long, and a half day on Saturday when work ceased at 2.00 pm, Walter's first tasks involved the rocking horses which remained among the firm's best-known products, despite the extensive diversification which had occurred. Their manufacture was a highly skilled process, fitting legs of English beech into a well-seasoned Scandinavian pine torso and then mounting the completed body onto sturdy ash rockers. Most demanding of all was the shaping of the heads, done to a general template but always varying in detail because they were handmade. Carved in slack periods and allowed to cure beneath a mixture of glue, whitening and size, the horses were later rubbed down before several more coats of paint and a varnish finish were applied together with the final trappings such as saddlery. As a novice, Walter's initial contributions were rather less demanding but did include the unpleasant task of cleaning raw cow tails which were then cured and transformed into tails for the rocking horses. Such was the pressure of demand at Christmas time that employees were often required to work through until midnight – all this for a wage which, in Walter's case, was initially ten shillings (50p) a week. As if this was not enough, Walter also spent some time in the business's subsidiary factory, Allen and Co. (acquired in 1886), learning the intricacies of making baby carriages and prams, goods which contributed significantly to turnover. Such time as remained was taken up with evening classes in design at the Camden School of Art, and in building, carpentry and cabinet making at the Northern Polytechnic.

One of the boys' other tasks was to help with loading the vans which carried the firm's products direct to retailers, for while G. & J. had originally supplied wholesalers, the practice was subsequently abandoned, partly because the wholesalers demanded too high a profit margin and partly because Lines' generally bulky goods required too much storage space. The numerous retail outlets supplied by Lines included many of the new department stores brought into existence by the nation's rising purchasing power. In London, Harrods Stores Ltd. catered primarily for the top end of the booming consumer demand, while Gamages – as its clever strapline of 'the people's emporium' suggests – sought to draw in a wider range of customers and was particularly known for its well-stocked toy department. George and Joseph Lines obviously had an instinctive feel for these social differences and tailored their products accordingly. Thus the 1895–6 catalogue listed no fewer than seven sizes of rocking horse, the smallest of which was nineteen inches high and sold for 6/1d (about 30p) if of ordinary quality, but 9/6d (47½p) with extra carving, 12/6d (62½p) if supplied with polished rockers and a special finish, and 14/- (70p) if covered with real skin. The basic model of the largest horse, which was forty-five inches high, sold at 53/- (£2.65) rising to 97/- (£4.85) for the top-of-the-range skin-covered version. Such an approach was quite common in the trade but few competitors matched the sheer variety of sizes and qualities produced by G. & J: the horse acquired from Cremer for one child of the 1890s certainly seemed a very poor beast by comparison – 'two simple green rockers and a brown hair coat'.[47] Lines' other products were similarly available in a variety of sizes and prices. The 1895 catalogue showed seven sizes of wooden railway engines, together with four sizes of polished elm wheelbarrows and eight cheaper ones in painted pine. By 1903, eighteen versions of the builder's cart were in the list. Although there was some was some standardisation, for example in the undercarriages used for the various carts and trolleys, much was still hand finished, often to specifications provided by individual customers since a bespoke option was always offered.

If rocking horses and other heavy wooden items associated with transport in the broadest sense provided the staple output, additional lines were introduced fairly regularly, although the catalogues could be misleading in that items were sometimes described as new when they had in fact been available for some time, while illustrations could remain unchanged long after products had been updated or modified. The lack of a systematic numbering system further complicated matters with the 1903 catalogue, for example, containing five instances where the same number was applied to more than one toy. Nevertheless, the brothers could be innovative and were usually alert to new market opportunities. They enjoyed particular success in 1887 when they produced a Jubilee Hobby horse to mark Queen Victoria's half century on the throne, and at about the same time a new safety rocker, shamelessly 'borrowed' from an American invention, also appeared in the catalogue: by 1910 eight versions were available. Patents were registered for a Cherubs car and a bamboo bedstead, respectively in 1895 and 1896, while the first in a new range of dolls' houses competed in a segment of the market traditionally dominated by German makers.

The pace of innovation seemed to pick up even more as Queen Victoria's long reign finally gave way to a new century and a new monarch whose coronation afforded another commercial opportunity, exploited by Lines in the form of a massive pull-along locomotive and saloon carriage based on Edward VII's royal train. The well-established range of velocipede horses – a horse body attached to an early form of tricycle – was extended in 1905 to include a version for children aged 3 to 6. A three-wheeled foot cycle (an early version of the scooter) arrived in seven versions in 1903, accompanied by the first two Lines' pedal cars for children. The wheels, chassis and bodies for these products drew on the skills of Allen's coachbuilders, painters and upholsterers, which were easily transferable from pram making. Within a few years there were nine varieties of pedal car available for children, allowing the firm to capitalise on the growing popularity of the motor car among the social elites by describing itself, with some justification, as a pedal-powered motor manufacturer. As with the babies' and dolls' prams, the basic bodies were made in quantity, but the number of variations initially available meant that individual models were rarely finished until orders had actually been received. By 1913, the number of cars had risen to twenty-nine including, from 1911, hand-propelled versions in which the rear wheels were driven by a chain connected to two levers alternately pushed and pulled by the 'driver'. Prices ranged from 32/- (£1.60) to 278/- (£13.90) for the top range version of the Daimler Silver Knight, introduced in 1912, by which time all models had benefitted from the introduction of lighter bodies and stronger axles.

Velocipedes had long been a popular G. & J. product but, as with the firm's other wheeled toys, there were significant developments in the Edwardian years, especially after the Startler cycle was introduced in 1905. New dolls' prams were also added to the existing lines, while between them Will and Walter designed so many new models that by

1911 the catalogue included twenty-seven baby carriages and twenty-eight pushchairs, almost all of them available in varying specifications. Thereafter rationalisation took place in that twenty models were grouped together into the 'Ordinary' range, available usually in only a couple of colour variants, with a smaller number marketed as 'Extra Special XL'. Similarly, by 1911 most of the firm's toy mail carts had been redesigned and the number of models reduced to seven as opposed to the forty-six available in 1903. As with most of their wooden toys, the greater use of beech and elm gave Lines a qualitative edge over many other manufacturers who tended to use cheaper pine timbers.

A similar pattern of development was discernible with the range of dolls' houses. The 1902 and 1903 catalogues listed eighteen different types, most of them variations of the basic design first produced in the 1890s. But after being supplemented by models with more up-to-date styles, the whole lot was brought together in 1911 as a single range of eleven Fancy Villas, all (except the cheapest) utilising specially designed wallpapers and containing curtains and fireplaces. Among the available extras were a running water system, electric lights, bells and lifts, few of which were then widely available in real houses. The following year saw the introduction of a much cheaper set of half a dozen simpler, smaller-scale models costing between 3/2d (almost 17p) and 15/- (75p) and offering less variation in their exterior details. It is possible that this innovation was a direct response to reduced orders from Gamages, which had recently been replacing their Lines' houses with cheaper types imported from Germany. More generally though, as the chief buyer for Faudels, one of London's largest toy wholesalers, later explained, German manufacturers simply could not compete with the quality of products produced by firms such as Lines, even without taking into account the additional burden of freight costs.[48]

This emphasis on quality toys, widely acknowledged in the press and evidenced by their extensive presence in prominent retail outlets, ensured that Lines' goods found a ready market among the social elites of Edwardian Britain. The price of the most expensive certainly put them beyond the reach of the average pocket, but their availability in cheaper price ranges, combined with their prestige and the sheer power of social emulation did make them accessible to growing numbers of working and middle-class children whose parents had benefitted from three decades of rising real incomes. By 1909, the average weekly earnings of a miner and an engineer, for instance, stood respectively at about 32/- (£1.60) and 38/- (£1.90).[49] Salaries for clerical workers varied hugely between regions and occupations, but if many were worse off than coal miners, some such as those working for the London and County Bank or the General Hydraulic Power company received over £150 a year.[50] At all events, by 1907 G. & J.'s annual turnover had reached some £55,000, the equivalent today of more than £6,700,000.[51] This at least was the figure mentioned by Walter Lines when he gave evidence to a government inquiry in 1922, and it is consistent with surviving company accounts which show a turnover of more than £64,000 in 1913.[52]

But if Lines thus benefitted from rising disposable incomes in the domestic market, its goods were also enjoying overseas success. Although there are valid reasons for challenging claims about German dominance of the contemporary British toy market, it is indisputable that before 1914 Germany was the world's largest exporter of children's playthings. Yet it is often overlooked that on the eve of the First World War, Britain's own toy manufacturers sold some £629,000 of toys overseas, over half of them to the empire, especially India, Canada, Australia and South Africa. Lines contributed significantly to this figure, trading extensively within the empire, but also exporting to Europe, even Germany itself. Walter Lines was very proud of this latter fact, pointing out that the firm had good connections in leading German cities and was able to compete successfully with its most directly comparable German competitor, Hugo Reuthner who, like Lines, employed about 300 people in 1914. Here, as at home, G. & J. attributed its success to a combination of quality and price, as the prewar catalogues claimed:

> No one from the Colonies or Abroad interested in Toys will overlook the fact that we are the originators of the Strong English Toy and are years ahead in Finish, Design and Durability, and when prices are compared we are lowest every time. Then the years of experience we have had in packing

these goods tends to economy and freedom from breakage and we can give prompt delivery owing to our large output.

There are few large cities in the world today to which our Toys are not shipped.

The whole of this trade has come into being from recommendation of our Goods by satisfied buyers. We have not spent a penny in advertising our Goods abroad.[53]

It may be that Lines' commercial success in the first decade or so of the new century, and the apparent outburst of creativity and innovation on which it largely rested, was connected with George's retirement. His original dynamism seems rather to have atrophied with the passage of time and there had been friction with his brother, with Joseph telling his daughter Mary on one occasion that he had 'struggled to keep friendly with your uncle all those years'.[54] Certainly when George brought his partnership with Joseph to an end in 1903, there was disagreement about the value of the divisible assets and the final settlement was not entirely amicable.[55] It is equally likely, however, that the business was energised by the coming of age of the next generation. Will Lines was something of a motoring enthusiast and may have inspired the move to pedal cars. Walter had revealed, whether intuitive or learned, both a marked talent for toy design and a shrewd business acumen. Between them the pair were largely responsible for much of the innovation and redesigning characteristic of these years. Joseph seems to have recognised as much, and when he reached his sixtieth birthday in 1908 he transferred the assets to a limited liability company, capitalised at £24,000. It was a prudent measure, given the size of the enterprise and its success. He also made provision for the later transfer of some of the company's assets to Walter and Will. In 1910, they each received 501 of the £1 shares and were designated as joint managing directors, with Will also nominated as company secretary and Joseph continuing to serve as chairman. As for the other two sons, George went his own way, serving an apprenticeship in Lincoln as an electrical engineer while Arthur, barely out of his teens, joined the family firm as an apprentice in 1909. His terms of employment, penned personally by Joseph, made it clear that like his older brothers he could expect no preferential treatment. He was required to open the factory promptly at 7.55 am each morning, inspect the premises and report anything out of the ordinary before taking his place at the work bench. At closing time, he was responsible for ensuring all windows were shut, all electricity and gas turned off, and all fires safe. Like Walter and Will before him, he was also expected to attend art school and the polytechnic. His wage was set at 20/- (£1.00) a week, rising over two years to 30/- (£1.50) after which it was to be reviewed according to his efficiency and ability. At all times, Joseph stressed, Arthur was to act as though he was working for promotion and responsibility.[56]

The influence of the new management arrangements was soon apparent, for the sons' highly practical education had not blinded them to commercial realities in an increasingly competitive market place. Consciously or not they seem to have shared the belief, increasingly entertained by other contemporary British businessmen, that old practices and structures needed to change in response. Thus, in 1908, a company trade mark – a thin, stamped tinplate thistle emblem attached to most of their larger goods which had been spasmodically used for some time – was formally registered. This was an eminently sensible decision in an age when the copying of designs and products was widespread and difficult to prevent: among Lines' toy-making peers, both Frank Hornby and William Britain had to resort to the courts to protect themselves against makers of pirated products. The sons' influence was apparent, too, in the rationalisation and more professional appearance of the annual catalogues after 1910. Furthermore, the new managing directors not only understood the need for the continuous refreshment of products but also seemed to have grasped, if only instinctively, that it was not efficient to offer so many variants of individual items: hence the observable tendency in the years before the war towards some standardisation and reductions in the variations of finish on offer. For example, by 1913 the twenty-six prams in the catalogue were obtainable in only two colours. Each pedal car was similarly advertised as available in only two standard colours, although the long list of optional extra equipment survived. Again, the cheapest and dearest of the twenty dolls' prams in the 'Ordinary' range were now differentiated only by externals such as decoration, finish and upholstery.

Above all, however, the new managing directors were frustrated by the limits imposed on further expansion by their restricted factory space. Over the years, additional premises had been acquired or rented; the North Road Cattle market just before the turn of the century, then the buildings and yard of the London General Omnibus Company and Carlo Gatti's ice works opposite the Caledonian Road facility. Herein, however, lay a potential source of friction. Joseph did not share his sons' aspirations to move the enterprise on from what Walter later described rather disparagingly as a 'hotch potch of five little factories in North London whose small capacity and lack of convenience made them quite a hindrance even in those days.'[57] Emboldened perhaps by their enhanced status as shareholders, and the success of their new products, Walter and Will argued for the building of a new factory. Joseph, however, could see little reason to change a business which had done so well financially and had certainly enabled him to realise his stated ambition of providing 'affluence and comfort' for his seven children.[58] He remained, as Walter observed, a tough old Victorian who basically believed that 'rocking horses were the end of the toy business', and most of the innovative drive by now certainly appeared to be coming from his sons.[59] True, Joseph had moved on from his original habit of personally handing out weekly wages and then dividing any surplus between the firm (his left-hand trouser pocket) and himself (his right-hand trouser pocket) but some of his business practices remained rather archaic, notably the persistence of the bespoke side of the business. He was especially reluctant to endorse what he perceived to be unnecessary additional expenditure. Even in 1910 the firm's local deliveries were still being made by horse-drawn van because he would not invest in motorised transport. In 1911 he refused to pay for the photographic plates his sons wished to include in the current catalogue alongside the more traditional line drawings. Naturally enough, however, the next generation had an eye to the future and was particularly concerned that in the long run split-site operations would prove a burden in what was fast becoming an increasingly competitive manufacturing environment. As Walter put it to Joseph:

> We have a position among the leading manufacturers and we do not want to lose it. But we must not forget, our competitors are also going ahead. Why then handicap ourselves? We can maintain and improve our position but not under present conditions. Let us then take courage and proceed on the urgently necessary step of concentrating all our factories on one site.[60]

His concerns were not altogether unfounded. There were complaints from important stores such as Whiteleys and Bentalls about errors and late delivery of their orders while the Harrods business was lost altogether. A. W. Gamage was equally fed up, but proved more resourceful, dispatching one of his own (motorised) vans to pick up his delayed orders. Without telling their father, Walter and his brothers came up with a blueprint for a new factory, got a quote for building it and even identified several acres of railway land at Tottenham as a potential site which, because it was further out of London, would be cheaper to run. With the advantages of a single location and one floor, more machinery could be brought in generating, they calculated, a fifty per cent increase in production. When Walter presented both the case for a new factory and the model of it, which he had built himself, Joseph was furious that he had not been consulted, especially as his sons expected him, as the major shareholder, to bear the costs, and were threatening to resign if they did not get their way. Reacting angrily to this pistol at his head he threatened to sack Will, but after some acrimonious legal wrangling and on his part, perhaps, a very grudging acknowledgement that the business did need to look to the future rather than remain wedded to the past, he acquiesced. But the whole episode upset him greatly and he wrote with some feeling to his daughter Mary about his sons' ingratitude which he said, 'stabbed me to the core, they have conspired to wreck the whole affair as the whole three have written out their resignations after entering into contracts which must be paid for.'[61] But even his own wife Jane supported her boys' plans and had little sympathy for him, telling Walter that in wishing her husband a happy birthday in 1914 she had suggested that the best celebration would be a reconciliation with his sons.[62]

In a way these tensions between Joseph and his sons were something of a microcosm of what was happening within British industry generally at the time when, in the words of one authority, 'progressive thinking was beginning to make an impact on traditional attitudes, cracking the hardened surface of a business culture fashioned in much different conditions.'[63] The notion that indigenous entrepreneurship somehow failed in these years, especially in long-established industries bound by tradition and reluctant to change entrenched and hitherto successful practices, has a long pedigree among historians. But one of the most powerful counter-arguments lies in the dynamism apparent in some newer sectors, especially retailing and light consumer industries, which of course included toys. Both attitudes were evident within G. & J. The father's reluctance to invest much in marketing, publicity or more efficient plant may certainly be seen as a personification of complacency born of past success while his sons' aspirations to embrace the opportunities for expansion offered by rising living standards, new technologies and mass advertising were an embodiment of entrepreneurial vigour.

It was Walter who oversaw the construction of the new modern factory. It was, commented a reporter in the *Toy and Fancy Goods Trader*, a 'pleasure to see such a perfectly arranged and organised factory' run by a firm whose products were 'so renowned as to create demand for them from all parts of the world.'[64] Separated from the showrooms in order to minimise the fire insurance premiums, manufacturing took place in a series of contiguous process shops, all powered by electricity and connected to each other by an internal telephone system. Completed goods were then subject to a final quality check before their dispatch, in the company's own transport if the destination was within a fifty-mile radius of London, or to more distant parts via the railway sidings adjacent to the plant. For the comfort of employees, there was also a central heating system fuelled by wood waste and improved cloakroom facilities. By the time the new factory was ready for occupation G. & J. had some 300 workers, fewer than Frank Hornby's Meccano operation in Liverpool, but about the same size as Bassett-Lowke's model engine enterprise and larger than most other leading toy manufacturers. The soft toy maker, Farnell, for example, had 240 employees at this time, Britains employed 270 to make its toy soldiers, while Chad Valley and Roberts Brothers had 280 and 201 workers respectively on their books.[65]

But the Lines' workforce barely had time to familiarise itself with the new plant before the settled political and economic world of the long nineteenth century was shattered by the outbreak of world war. The initial expectation was for a brief conflict and few anticipated its duration, its horrendous casualty rates, or its sweeping economic and social effects on civilian life. Although, like most businesses, Lines lost employees in the initial rush of enthusiastically patriotic volunteers to the colours, for a few months at least it remained very much business as usual. Indeed, *The Times* suggested that the hostilities provided British toy makers with a unique opportunity to fill the gap left in the home market by the sudden cessation of German imports.[66] This view was certainly prevalent in government circles, and as early as September 1914 the Board of Trade organised an exhibition of German toys to indicate what might henceforth be manufactured in Britain. The following year, toy making was one of the five sectors officially designated to participate in the first ever British Industries Fair (BIF), an initiative to encourage the specified industries to plug the gaps left by the drying up of German imports and to develop new overseas markets. Invitations to attend were thus extended not to the general public but to wholesalers and overseas buyers. The venture certainly achieved its first objective as far as toys were concerned, for the outcome was a veritable eruption of new businesses, which took their place at the fair alongside the older and well-established firms. *The Times* noted that most of the 100 or so toy exhibitors were introducing new lines, although some were displaying traditional 'strong and expensive' items.[67] The latter included the rocking horses to which Lines gave top billing in its BIF catalogue entry, although its thirty-nine lines of text, one of the longest in the entire document, did cover many of the firm's other products, including a few new ones. Unlike many others, G. & J. showed little inclination to turn generally to war toys, although the addition of a camouflage green superstructure did serve to transform a basic pedal car chassis into the Lion toy battleship at six guineas (£6.30). Among other 'new' items was a foot cycle or scooter, an idea probably originating in America, although a three-wheeled foot cycle had first been listed in the catalogue as early as 1903. More striking perhaps, was the promise of an electrically powered car for children, although at £35 it was never going to command significant sales.

The Board of Trade deemed the BIF sufficiently successful to warrant repeating in subsequent years, and the civil servants' optimism was apparently shared in the G. & J. boardroom. At all events, the Lines' list for the 1915–16 season was the most ambitious to date, containing four full pages of colour photographs. The contents, however, reflected the simmering tensions among the directors. The front sections were given over to the traditional products to which Joseph apparently remained firmly wedded – rocking horses, velocipedes, and pole horses. Later pages looked more to the future, as instanced by the announcement of The New Sporting Car, much lighter than previous pedal cars on account of its tubular steel chassis and curved laminated wooden body. However, almost before the catalogue was available to the trade, Lines had lost one of its leaders, with Walter enlisting in the Territorial Honorable Artillery Company in October 1915 and subsequently going on to serve in France and Italy. The Army also claimed Arthur who ultimately found himself attached to the Rifle Brigade on the western front. As a family man already in his thirties, Will was deemed too old to serve and was thus left to run the family business along with his father. It was a predictably uneasy collaboration. Serving segments of the domestic market largely uncontested by German toys, G. & J. was not much affected by competition from new firms hoping to capitalise on the absence of this foreign competition. It is true that the Board of Trade specifically encouraged a couple of newcomers, the Parkstone Toy Factory and the Happy Day Toy Company, to produce wooden toys while another company, Emell, diversified by adding dolls' houses to its existing product range, but none of the enterprises set up in response to the government's overtures were large enough to represent any sort of threat to a firm as large or as well known for quality goods as Lines. Nor was there much cause to worry about the marked upsurge of imports from France, Japan and the USA, all trying to benefit from the fact that by 1915, German toy imports to Britain had shrivelled to virtually nothing compared to the £1,200,000 worth entering the country in the last full year of peace. These foreign products did not really compete with the types of toys in which Lines specialised and, in any case, after March 1916, Board of Trade restrictions virtually ended all toy importing except from France.

Far more problematic was the wholesale disruption of normal trade patterns which did eventually impact on Lines' exports and also interfered with domestic distribution as transport systems were increasingly prioritised towards the needs of the military and heavy industry. Overtons, a major dealer in Leeds, claimed in the autumn of 1915 to be buying toys from anyone except English makers because their deliveries had become so unreliable. A few months later, a trade journal stressed that buyers were less concerned about prices than about the manufacturers' inability to guarantee delivery of orders.[68] Furthermore, despite the official encouragement initially given to toy makers by government, the supply of raw materials became strained as the war dragged on, a situation in which the claims of non-essential industries were naturally given low priority. Thus, the official rationale for restricting the 1915 BIF to a few selected trades was said to be the maximisation of opportunities provided by the cessation of imports: by the following year, however, it had been reworded to avoiding 'interference with the production of munitions of war'.[69] Raw material accounted for a third of Lines' total expenditure in any one year, with a further third going to labour, and the rest being divided between overheads and profits. Once the company had exhausted its accumulated stocks of metals, timber and so on, scarcities and rising prices, as well as more expensive labour, began to impinge heavily. By March 1915, the cost of timber shelving, a key material both for the firm's products and the cases in which larger items were usually packed, had risen by some fifty-seven per cent. Things became even tougher after 1916 when Lloyd George replaced Asquith as prime minister and brought a far more dirigiste approach to the conduct of the war. In the spring of 1917, an order in council gave the Army total possession of certain grades of soft woods, while all timber sales were subjected to a strict licensing procedure. In the same year, metal supplies to all but strategic industries were effectively halted, although combined action by the toy makers did secure a small concession in this respect. In 1918, restrictions were imposed on the supply of turpentine and lead, two essential ingredients of the paints with which Lines' heavy wooden toys were usually finished. Walter Lines' written evidence to a postwar departmental committee suggested that, over the course of the war, G. & J.'s raw material costs per unit went up by eighty per cent.[70] Finally, of course, there was a continuous drain of manpower out of the labour force. Although some finishing work – sewing the textiles used in dolls' prams or decorating the dolls' houses, for instance – had been carried out by women, the lure of better paid work in other industries inevitably drew them away, while male labour was absorbed into the armed forces. Even the possibility of getting individual (usually highly skilled) workmen exempted from conscription was lost when, in the spring of 1918, the government included toy making in the list of trades automatically excluded from the exemption scheme.

With materials and skilled labour in short supply, it was inevitable that as the war dragged on G.& J.'s turnover would fall. After dipping in 1915 and then briefly recovering to its 1914 level, it declined steadily thereafter and by 1918 was down to £48,000. Over the same period, the firm's annual wage bill fell from almost £14,500 in 1914 to about £9,300, a reduction of more than a third.[71] The high quality for which Lines' toys had been renowned also suffered and Walter admitted that 'customers of the old firm were thoroughly fed up with the poor stuff they had been forced to buy during the war.'[72] Joseph Lines' only response to these difficulties was to hike up his prices – it was after all a seller's market – and to maintain very healthy dividend payments for the shareholders (ie his family), seven per cent until 1916, eight per cent in 1917 and a massive ten per cent in 1918. Additionally, despite his participation in the BIF, he did not care to involve himself in the industry more widely. Walter had attended the inaugural meeting in 1915 of what became the Association of Toy Manufacturers and

Wholesalers (ATMW), but Joseph showed no interest in a body intended to protect the interests of the trade in turbulent times despite, or perhaps because of, the prominence of his own firm. But with the war drawing to a close, and with one eye on the future, Will was frustrated by his father's conservatism and complacency, even more so perhaps because advancing years had done nothing to modify his parent's authoritarian tendencies. More than once Will told Walter that they would not be able to continue working with Joseph when peace returned and, in fact, he did begin to look for a place where they could set up on their own. Walter initially tried to discourage his brother from acting too hastily, still hopeful perhaps that the gulf could be bridged and Joseph would be persuaded to forgive his sons fully for their insistence on shifting to the new factory in 1914. He hoped in vain.

Chapter Two

Going Solo, 1918–1929

By the time hostilities ended in November 1918, the war had long since descended into a bloody hell of mud, misery and machinery, far removed from the brief and glorious cavalry charge to Berlin envisaged by some in Britain when it began four years earlier. Millions had been killed and many millions more were soon to perish in the influenza epidemic, which swept the globe from the spring of 1918 into 1919. If Britain had avoided the physical damage which so scarred parts of western Europe, the country certainly paid a high enough price in terms of manpower losses, the liquidation of international investment to fund its war effort and the running down of capital equipment, not to mention the consistent raising of postwar expectations in order to sustain civilian morale. Restoring the pattern of prewar economic activity and satisfying the general population's anticipation of enhanced living standards were never going to be quick or straightforward, and against such a backcloth the establishment of a new toy manufacturing enterprise appears trivial: as one government minister reportedly put it at the time in a somewhat mangled metaphor, 'the toy trade world and all that therein is melts into a very small potato when looked at through his spectacles.'[1] For Will Lines, however, that potato, no matter how insignificant in a global or national context, represented the future. Thoroughly disenchanted with Joseph's handling of the family business, he was resolved to strike out afresh. Walter's initial reservations soon vanished, and by the time he was demobilised even his commanding officer, Colonel Borwick, was aware that he intended to join Will.

Borwick knew this only because he had received a letter from Will urging that Walter's release from the Army be expedited as he was needed for their new business venture. The colonel, predictably perhaps described later by Walter as 'a first class man in every way', was sympathetic and Walter was officially discharged on 14 February 1919.[2] In replying to Will's correspondence, Borwick wrote that he could 'well understand why the family so urgently need Walter's organising ability to sort matters out at home', a comment which helps explains why Walter, originally enlisted as a driver, had risen to the rank of captain and was currently serving as the colonel's adjutant.[3] So confident was Borwick of his subordinate's capabilities that he even offered to invest £3,000 in the new business. Arthur, who was also committed to the venture, had had an equally successful military career and at the time of his demobilisation was an acting company sergeant major in the Rifle Brigade. The remaining brother, George, had not previously been involved in the family firm and still showed no inclination to join his siblings. Wounded at Armentières in February 1916, he was not discharged from Royal Engineers until April 1919 and then opted to try his hand at farming. This rather disappointed Joseph who had harboured hopes of utilising George's engineering skills by setting him up in a nearby factory to provide metal parts for G. & J. But his vexation with George was nothing compared with his anger when he discovered that his other three sons were intent on establishing their own independent business: he promptly barred his wife, their mother, from seeing them.

They were undeterred, however, and even before Walter got out of the Army, Will had already had one approach for a factory in Clapham rebuffed. By March 1919, however, they had identified an equally promising possibility in Ormside Street off the Old Kent Road. The owners of the Hatcham Works were willing to sell the entire assets of their woodworking business – land, buildings, plant, and timber stocks, together with a number of horse-drawn and motorised vans. Will sold his house to raise the funds necessary for the deposit on the freehold of the premises, while Arthur and Walter contributed such savings as they had been able to accumulate, some perhaps derived from their shares in the old family business. With sales down to some £40,000 G. & J. paid no dividend at all in 1919, but prior to 1914 the brothers' shares had earned each of them between £20 and £30 annually, a return which grew during the war years with the dividend climbing to ten per cent by 1918. But having closed a deal which committed them to £15,000 for the works, and several additional thousands for plant and stock, considerable sums remained to be found. At this juncture Will ran into difficulties with his bank, which proved disinclined to lend against the security of leasehold premises. Ralph Freeman, a rising star in the international engineering firm of Douglas Fox and Partners, and who had married Joseph's daughter Mary in 1908, thought that Will had been treated abominably. He wrote:

> Unless you change, I personally feel that the burden of a bank that is a drag upon you will be so serious that your chances of success are gravely diminished... . The attitude of your man in this matter makes my blood boil. He is one of the muddlers that stop this country making any progress.

He even suggested that if Will did not follow his advice and find another more accommodating bank, he might withdraw his own promised investment of £2,000 in the new company.[4]

Yet Will's experience was by no means uncommon. In July 1917, the *Toyshop and Fancy Goods Journal* had carried a letter from another toy maker who had secured an order worth £1,500 from a wholesaler, only to find that his bank would not put up the funds to enable him to produce on the necessary scale.[5] A few months later, the store proprietor A. W. Gamage asserted bluntly in an interview that because 'British bankers have never financed brains', the best means of encouraging manufacturers to invest in plant and equipment was to impose tariffs on imports.[6] The alleged reticence of banks to finance manufacturing industry is a well-explored theme in British economic history, but the general consensus is that the charge is not proven and certainly the Lines brothers had more success when they approached Lloyds Bank in Lombard Street.[7] Even so, its manager was initially cautious, asking bluntly why he should lend £28,000 to mere toy makers. According to his son, Walter answered by rolling up his sleeves and showing his well-worn working hands.[8] The story may well have been somewhat embroidered as it passed down the family over the years, but the manager must have appreciated that his potential clients had worked for a long time in one of the sector's leading firms, in the process acquiring valuable practical and commercial experience, establishing important contacts and also overseeing the removal of an entire enterprise into new dedicated premises. Furthermore, Walter had a high personal standing in the trade more generally. He had represented G. & J. at the inaugural meeting of the ATMW in 1915, was currently its vice chairman and a member of its manufacturers' committee, and was shortly to become chairman (in March 1922). Overall, the brothers' credibility was such that a few months later a trade journal suggested that any business in which they were the principals 'was bound to make its mark'.[9] At all events, the Lloyds manager was persuaded, they got their money and Lines Brothers Ltd. was formally incorporated on 1 May 1919.

Under the Articles of Association, Arthur, Will and Walter all became life directors with the latter pair acting jointly as managing directors. George Campbell, an accountant and soon to be their brother-in-law by virtue of his marriage to another of their sisters, and R. C. Munro, an old school friend and member of a well-known engineering business, were appointed as non-executive directors: they were later joined on the board by Ralph Freeman when he returned from overseas. The business was initially capitalised at £50,000, divided into 47,500 preference shares of £1 and 50,000 ordinary shares at 1/- (5p) each. The brothers' confidence in their future success was evident in their agreement that for every ordinary share bought by a preference shareholder they would buy five. On this basis £37,087 was raised from family and friends including Colonel Borwick and Ralph Freeman: a few shares were taken by some employees such as Robert Garner, a former soldier who worked briefly for Lines as a draftsman and designer.[10]

The partners moved in to the Hatcham Works gradually, as the previous owners vacated it in stages, and not until 6 June 1919 were they in full possession. But by planning the layout and equipment of the various departments in advance, they were able to undertake structural alterations and plant installation as soon as an area was empty, thereby minimising delays between occupation and the start of actual manufacturing. New equipment was installed and the sale of unwanted plant brought in over £5,500, much more than the £3,000 expected, and a welcome addition to their start-up funds. In this way they quickly established a factory containing some sixty-eight wood and metal-working machines, spray painting equipment, and a stove enamelling plant, together with dedicated rooms for drying off varnished goods and bare timber. Retention of the existing workforce had been part of the terms of sale, but while this certainly enabled production to start as early as mid-May, well before occupation and re-equipment had been completed, it soon became apparent that not all the existing employees were amenable to the more rigorous work regime which was imposed. A good number were dismissed, to be replaced by a mix of school leavers and experienced tradesmen, including a few former G. & J. employees. Some of these had actually been poached from their father's business well before the new firm was even incorporated, with one man writing as early as 22 March 1919 to inform Will that he was leaving G. & J. the following Saturday and would be pleased to start his new job at Lines Brothers as soon as was convenient.[11]

But if the labour force was expected to work hard in a factory that was both old and cold, it was relatively well rewarded. The heads of the various departments received a salary plus a commission on their section's monthly output, giving them a powerful motive to maintain high output levels. For shop-floor workers the incentive came from the use of a piece work system. Even though the calculation of process times was quite crude and sometimes rather arbitrary, an average man could make £5 for a forty-eight-hour week and the most productive could earn even more. Contemporary information about wages in the industry is scarce and the absence of unionisation meant that levels varied widely. Nevertheless, surviving data suggest that the Lines' rates were generous compared say with skilled bench workers and sawyers at Chiltern Toys, who respectively made 62/- (£3.10) and 70/- (£3.50) a week in 1918.[12] Lines' wages were certainly well above the 64/- (£3.20) set for adult males in June 1921, when national rates for the industry were formulated by the newly created Toy Trade Board. Furthermore, as Will reported to the 1920 AGM, the board was already proposing to take out a group insurance, which would be cheaper for the workers than the existing ordinary industrial insurance, and also to introduce a paid week's holiday. While this latter benefit was not unique to Lines at the time, it is worth noting that legislation granting it to all British workers as a *legal* right was not passed until 1938.

The Lines brothers may have demanded much of their employees but they led by example and also opted to draw very low salaries for the first few years of operations. Broadly speaking the intent was that Arthur, whose relative youthfulness and less overtly abrasive manner perhaps made him a more approachable presence than his brothers on the shop floor, should run the factory and the administrative side of the business. Will was in charge of sales while Walter provided the company's main creative energy, not least in designing and sometimes actually constructing prototypes for new toys. So fertile was his mind in this respect that even when he was 'much up in the air' following his engagement to Henrietta Hendrey early in 1920, he still found time to develop the idea for an aeroplane toy, which was essentially a pedal car with wings, rudder and propeller. 'It seemed a good moment,' he wrote rather laconically to his new fiancée.[13] In practice, however, during the early years all three did a bit of everything. Walter and Arthur moved in with Will and his wife in Blackheath to be closer to the factory and to facilitate their planning for its development. After long days on site, the directors would return to Blackheath and devote their evenings to the business as well. From these discussions there eventually emerged the firm's tri-angular trade mark bearing the logo 'Triangtois'. Although it well-symbolised the company's triune leadership, it was still a surprisingly French-sounding term for a business which, from the outset, stressed the essential Britishness of its products. Initially most pressing was the preparation of the inaugural catalogue, so urgent in fact that it was handwritten overnight and illustrated with pen sketches. When the first price list was issued in the summer it bore all the hallmarks of haste, with some items lacking basic information and others little more than ideas still on the drawing board. A strong element of product continuity from the old days was evident in the form of traditional painted wheelbarrows, hand cars, pole carts, push-along wheeled horses, a builder's tip cart, a wooden lorry, railway locomotives, and safety rocking horses, most of which were available in several sizes and finishes, another throwback to the familiar. But the emphasis was firmly on pedal cars (ten new models), pull-along vans and engines, dolls' houses and prams and, if again, there were resemblances to G. & J. products – the Victory pedal motor car was very similar to G. & J.'s Sporting Car – this was understandable given that Walter and his brothers had been largely responsible for many G. & J. designs in the first place.

Perhaps in an effort to distance itself from the old family firm, Lines Brothers made sure that the catalogues continuously made reference to improvement and innovation; the Hatcham car was said to be much stronger than other models, for instance, because it was constructed on a new principle (unfortunately unspecified!), while the dolls' motor car was 'far ahead of anything previously produced'.[14] When it finally came out, the list claimed to offer 'the best toys on the market. Beautifully made painted & finished.'[15] Walter in particular, it seems, was well aware of the importance of asserting quality as well as delivering it. A draft version of another early list in the Peggy Lines papers is covered in his pencilled annotations, all designed to emphasise the innate excellence of what was being offered. Thus he added 'splendid model bonnet' to the description of the Hatcham pedal car and the words 'especially fine model, nicely upholstered' to the blurb for the Mercury.[16] The stress on innovation and quality underlines the way in which Lines Brothers consciously played on the widespread disenchantment, evident among retailers and consumers alike, about the poor standard of toys that had been available in Britain during the war.

The new business made a promising start. A day after an office girl distributed the first handwritten list, an order worth £5,600 was placed by Harrods. Other former G. & J. customers were soon following suit, including Harvey, Greenacre & Co, a major South African department store based in Durban but with branches in several other large towns throughout the country. The export side of the business was fraught with difficulty, given currency fluctuations and the wholesale disruption of international trade patterns caused by the war, but that did not deter Lines Brothers. Inspired by this early success in South Africa, the company set about appointing agents in other likely overseas markets, making up mixed-case lots of toys for their trial orders. In marked contrast to Joseph's reluctance to publicise his products either at home or abroad, his sons backed up their export effort by advertising in the multilingual *British Standard Exporter*. Edited by E. Noel Baker, founder of a movement to encourage British exports, the paper offered advice on all aspects of selling abroad and was routinely found in Britain's overseas embassies and foreign chambers of commerce. A surviving copy from 1920 carried six pages from Lines Brothers, by far the largest of the advertisements placed by a number of toy companies.[17]

By Christmas 1919, and despite a brief strike by their moulders, Lines Brothers was already turning out 400 toy motor cars a week, prompting the *Toy and Fancy Goods Trader* to remark that it was doubtful 'if even their most optimistic well-wishers could have foreseen the remarkable developments which have taken place in the last six months.'[18] Two months later £40,000 worth of business was concluded at the BIF, and for much of 1920 new accounts were being opened at the rate of twenty to thirty a month. Output was extended to include not only traditional rocking horses and handcars but also a scooter, the Fairyscoot, which again closely resembled an earlier G. & J. design. Because it was constructed from tubular metal it was much stronger (and more expensive) than even the best wooden models previously available. The major success of 1920, however, was the highly innovative Fairycycle. Patented by Walter and tested by Will's small son, it visually resembled the Scooter on which it was based, but the addition of a saddle and pedals transformed it into a small-wheeled cycle. At five guineas (£5.25) it was quite expensive but proved so popular that within a couple of years longer production runs brought the price down to 75/- (£3.75). The actual manufacture was carried out by the Unique and Unity Cycle Company, a Birmingham-based engineering firm which the brothers knew well since it had long supplied wheels and tricycles to G. & J. Innovation also occurred on the baby carriage side of the business, where relatively consistent demand helped offset fluctuations in toy sales which were heavily concentrated around the Christmas period. Lines Brothers' newest models were not only more stable, thanks to the use of four small wheels of equal diameter giving prams a lower centre of gravity, but at the lower end so inexpensive as to make their purchase possible for a 'new and very extensive public':

this at least was according to the publicity for the 'Joy' model, which was claimed to be the cheapest in the world and was still offered in half a dozen colours.[19] Only raw material shortages in the first part of the year held the output of baby carriages down to 200 a week.

Within a year of its establishment, and on the back of this steadily expanding range of toys and prams, Lines claimed that it had already become the largest maker of its class of goods in the UK. Will's satisfaction was apparent at the first AGM in 1920 when he reported that the company had received 'many congratulations from customers on the good finish and improved designs of our products', £12,000 worth of which had been delivered in July alone.[20] Walter, who alternated annually with Will as company chairman, was not tempted into complacency, however. Maintaining such a level of business, he said, would mean orders of £144,000 over the next year, but added that he would be disappointed if that figure was not exceeded. His statement neatly encapsulated the company's straightforward focus on raising turnover and profits on a continuous basis. Walter's hopes were fully realised (as Table 1 indicates). In its first four years Lines Brothers' turnover tripled to reach almost £223,000, which was even more remarkable considering that over the same period the issued capital rose by just £10,275.

Table 1: Statement Showing Progress of Lines Brothers Ltd. from Commencement (to nearest £)

Year to	Capital issued (£)	Net Turnover (£)	Net profit (£)	Preference share dividend (%)	Ordinary share dividend (%)
30 June 1920	36,088	76,992	5,709	8	100
30 June 1921	39,556	137,656	7,447	8	100
30 June 1922	43,081	179,262	18,219	8	300
30 June 1923	46,363	222,860	22,167	8	400

Source: Museum of Childhood (MOC). P. Lines Archive. Uncatalogued. Statement showing progress of Lines Brothers Ltd. from commencement. Cyclostyled copy.

This impressive performance was the outcome of extensive advertising, lower prices facilitated by increasing mechanisation, the expansion of the product ranges and continuous improvements in their specifications and designs. One important innovation in baby carriages, for instance, was the introduction of the closed end design in 1921 whereby the side and end panels of the body formed a single complete shell. As for dolls' prams, there were no fewer than nineteen in the 1922 catalogue, along with twenty-seven different types of dolls' houses. That year also saw the introduction of a new series of pull-along wooden engines to replace the motley selection offered in the first catalogue, and in 1923 milk floats and milk lorries, both familiar sights in city streets, were added to an already impressive range of wooden motor vehicles. The increased availability of better-quality plywood permitted improvements in the bodies of most pedal cars, which rolled out of the factory in great quantities and under a variety of high-sounding marques – improved versions of 1919 models such as the Canterbury and the Mercury, the York, the Prince, the Torpedo, the Chitty Bang, the Duplex and so on. Their prices ranged widely, for the cheapest were little more than simple painted bodies on wheeled frames with pedals. Top-end models were far more sophisticated and realistic in appearance, thanks to the addition of numerous refinements such as luggage racks and trunks, working lamps and horns, windscreens, driving mirrors, plated radiators, petrol cans, tool boxes, adjustable seats, hoods, opening bonnets and even dummy engines.

The appeal of product ranges offering a variety of prices to suit all pockets was further enhanced by the fact that Lines also took more care than was customary with packing its goods for delivery. For years there had been complaints that British toy makers did not pay sufficient attention to this side of their businesses, with the result that wholesalers, retailers and consumers often received goods which had been damaged or had lost components in transit. Such grumbles were a recurring theme in the trade press, unfavourable comparisons frequently being drawn with the superior practices of German or Japanese manufacturers.[21] Lines sought to redress this by introducing fibreboard cartons, a decision that seems to have been decisive in securing the first order from South Africa. The new cartons were not only lighter than traditional wooden crates and thus cheaper to transport, but because some toys were specifically designed to fit the cartons – some of the items being collapsible – the possibility of damage during carriage was much reduced. The new packaging featured prominently in the company's publicity which emphasised the high levels of customer satisfaction it produced. Even though the 1922 sets of dolls' house furniture were marketed on the basis that they were cheaper than the costlier ranges because they lacked some of the fine detail, the advertisements still stressed the fact that they were 'packed splendidly'.[22]

Although all three of the brothers were well known in the trade because of their previous association with G. & J., unlike their father they fully understood the importance of consistently bringing their business and its products to the notice of the buying public. They had, after all, served their apprenticeships at the end of the nineteenth century when entrepreneurs such as William Lever and Thomas Lipton were building highly successful operations in part at least by exploiting the publicity opportunities provided by the burgeoning popular press. With newspaper circulations booming even more spectacularly in the postwar years, it was no surprise that within a few months of Lines Brothers' launch, mass advertisements for its products appeared in the *Daily Mail*, the *News Chronicle*, and the *Daily Mirror*, publications which had a combined circulation of more than 3,000,000 by 1921. At the same time, material placed in the trade press ensured that retailers – Lines had no truck with wholesalers – were fully stocked with, and well informed about, new products when customers came into their shops. The initial success of this approach ensured that it became something of norm, especially in the pre-Christmas season. It was the obvious way to bring new products, such as the Fairycycle, to the public attention while retailers appreciated handling toys with which consumers had already been familiarised through the national press.[23] Like most other major toy companies, Lines Brothers also exhibited (very prominently) at the annual BIF and the trade fairs, which provided an important platform for the launch of new products. The whole selling effort was backed up by travelling salesmen and it was a further indication of the company's rapid early growth that the team of three appointed in 1919 had expanded to seven by 1924.

Much of the early advertising material was characterised by rather excruciating word plays on the company name, such as 'Lines lines are selling lines', 'kiddies line up for Lines', 'Lines lines are straight lines', and 'Lines lines are novel lines'. There was an emphasis on their British origin, understandable at a time when German toys were beginning to reappear in shops, while the other most prevalent themes were realism and quality. As one 1920s advert had it: 'Children love toys which are replicas of the "real thing". These toys must be strong .... Lines Bros. Ltd. make the best it is possible to buy. They are finished in an excellent style, very strong and well made.'[24] The publicity for the 1922 BIF went even further, asserting bluntly that Lines Brothers made the world's best toys. This willingness to advertise and to keep retailers informed was in marked contrast to Joseph's rather dismissive attitude, since he had rarely bothered to advertise and had made a virtue of having no salesmen. The brothers certainly did not follow their father's example in these respects and while they had their own inherent business acumen, it may be that Walter in particular had learned much from Frank Hornby of Meccano Ltd. with whom he was very friendly, and who was something of an advertising genius.[25] Joseph, for his part, was quite derogatory about his sons' advertising efforts.[26]

That the company's turnover rose so much in such a short space of time was all the more remarkable given the disturbed trading environment in which it was operating. True, Lines Brothers was launched in the heady boom days following the restoration of peace in November 1918, when inflation together with the anticipation of a speedy return to prewar conditions and the realisation of the promised 'land fit for heroes' made for economic optimism. Even before the Armistice was signed, the 180 toy exhibitors at the 1918 BIF secured orders worth £500,000.[27] The following year, by which time an estimated 40,000 people were working in the industry, toy makers comprised the largest single group of the 570 firms showing at the fair. Yet within a couple of years the mood had changed dramatically as boom gave way to slump. British industry struggled to cope with the loss of established overseas markets, while the huge financial costs of the war proved a crippling burden and the morale-boosting promises made during the war evaporated in the harsh light of economic reality. Unemployment soared and while the older staple industries at the heart of Britain's economy were worst affected, few sectors escaped altogether. By 1922, it was claimed, eighty-two of the 300 toy manufacturers operating in 1919 had closed down and the survivors were employing a mere 5,000 people, a reduction of almost eighty-eight per cent in two years. It was perhaps to be expected that newer firms established during the emergency of war should have been worst hit. Thus the Woolstan Doll Company, which opened in 1915 with eighty workers, was reduced to only ten part-timers by 1921, while the 700 employees of the British Metal and Toy Manufacturers, formed in September 1914, all lost their jobs when the firm was liquidated in 1921. Less predictable, however, was the impact on some of the older prewar businesses, exacerbated from June 1921 by the requirement to pay wages centrally determined by the new trade board. It is true that the rates were steadily reduced, falling from an initial 64/- (£3.20) per forty-eight-hour week for adult men and 34/- (£1.70) for adult women, to 56/- (£2.80) and 30/- (£1.50) respectively by January 1922, with a further adjustment the following year taking them down to 50/- (£2.50) and 27/- (£1.35). Yet the burden was still too heavy: employment figures presented to a Board of Trade Inquiry in 1922 revealed that Chad Valley's workforce had fallen from 560 in 1920 to 410 by 1921. Roberts Brothers may have had more employees on its books in 1922 than previously, but they were working a twenty-four-hour week compared with over fifty-two hours in 1919. Lines Brothers was not much affected by the wage regulation because its use of piece rates meant that it had only about half a dozen workers earning the minimum sum prescribed by the trade board. Nevertheless Walter, who appeared as a main witness before the inquiry, claimed that he had done only £5,000 worth of business at the 1921 BIF compared with £40,000 the year before, and indicated that he, too, had been forced to lay off about half his workforce which was now down to about 250.[28]

The inquiry had been set up by the Board of Trade to adjudicate on an application from the ATMW to bring the toy industry under the aegis of the 1921 Safeguarding of Industries Act, allowing the imposition of tariffs on designated imports. The application rested on the claim – which was not without justification – that government had more or less promised in 1915 to protect the postwar toy industry in this way.[29] But import quotas on toys were eased within a few months of the war's end, and as early as August 1919, £73,000 worth of German toys entered Britain. In September the restrictions were removed entirely and by October the value of German imports had shot up to £159,000. Still enjoying the postwar boom, the manufacturers did not immediately react. Asked in late 1920 if Britain's toy makers would be adversely affected by the reappearance of German toys in the domestic market, a Lines Brothers spokesman replied that he was not anticipating any difficulty because German goods were poorly finished and its toy workers had just received a big wage increase.[30] There was perhaps a hint of complacency in his further assertion that the British public would not quickly forget the war, although by constantly stressing that it was a British firm Lines, like many of its peers, seemed loath to leave this to chance. Attitudes hardened dramatically, however, when the German mark collapsed, conferring a huge price advantage on German goods and, according to one manufacturer, costing the jobs of 22,500 British toy makers.[31] In a letter circulated at about the same time, the ATMW itself claimed that a third of businesses had closed, putting between 22,000 and 30,000 people out of work.[32]

Among the supporting papers submitted by the association to the Board of Trade was a list of prices and other information from individual manufacturers to show the scale of the problem. Lines Brothers was invited to provide the data with respect to wooden toys, but the firm's reply was pretty much confined to claiming that its selling costs had gone up eighty per cent since the war. That the response otherwise lacked substance confirms that the firm was still not unduly alarmed by rising German imports, few of which were serious competitors to its own range of products. Virtually the only exception was a set of Lines' dolls' house furniture, described by the inquiry chairman as being 'of very beautiful design'.[33] Customers, it was pointed out by counsel for the ATMW, were more likely to prefer cheap German furniture at 6d (2½p) a set rather than the same size Lines product at 14/- (70p). Certainly, when Walter appeared in person before the inquiry he did stress that the introduction of tariffs would enable his firm to expand at the cheaper end of market and add a further 200 to his workforce. Even more pertinently, though, he also referred to the indirect and immediate difficulty created for his business by the impact of German competition on some of his suppliers. In evidence, he produced a letter from the St Stephens works in Birmingham which made most of the thousands of wheels Lines needed but which had been forced to cut its workforce by half in the face of imported competition.

That counsel for the opposition to the ATMW application should devote a good portion of his closing statement to discrediting Walter's evidence was testimony to the weight conferred upon it by his long experience of the trade, the rapidity with which his new firm had developed and by his current role as the ATMW's vice chairman. The barrister's argument proved persuasive and the inquiry concluded by rejecting the application. Shortly afterwards Walter, already the public face of Lines Brothers, became chairman of the association, thereby becoming the public face of the whole trade as well and now in a position to shape it in accord with his own thinking. At the meeting which had established the ATMW in September 1915, he had argued strongly but unsuccessfully in favour of restricting membership to manufacturers. His attitude hardened still further in the years immediately after 1918 when the wholesalers generally proved indifferent to pleas from many quarters to buy British goods and then, profiting even more when the German mark collapsed, objected forcefully to the association's application for protection. Walter's remarks at the Board of Trade inquiry were thus highly critical, alleging that wholesalers generally took little part in the ATMW's work and were never friendly towards the manufacturers, which was why, he said, his own business bypassed them and dealt directly with the retail sector. Under Walter's prompting, the association reorganised itself in December 1922 along looser, sectional lines representing manufacturers, wholesalers and retailers. Lines Brothers was among the first of the fifty-two manufacturers who, by the following month, had applied to join the new Toy and Fancy Goods Trade Federation (TFGTF).

The disagreements within the trade over protection were soon subsumed in a much wider national debate when the new Conservative prime minister, Stanley Baldwin, called a general election in December 1923 on the basis that the only effective way to deal with mass unemployment was to introduce a general tariff on imports. The outcome was politically indecisive in that it resulted in a minority Labour government, but the economic result was very clear cut because protection was decisively rejected by the electorate. It made little difference to Lines Brothers, which continued to flourish, aided by a mild recovery in the economy which had already prompted the *Toy Trader* to claim in October 1923 that prospects for manufacturers were the most favourable for years.[34] Turnover in the trade year ending June 1923 reached almost a quarter of a million pounds as new products continued to appear alongside improved versions of existing toys and prams. Baby prams, which previously had had no identifiable brand, were brought together in 1922 under the new name of Pedigree, a choice allegedly inspired by a visit to brother George's farm on which he was raising pedigree pigs. Under this label quality was improved as more and better materials became available. Shock absorbers were added to the tubular chassis, and by 1925 the closed end design had been extended to many other models. Triangtois prams for dolls followed a similar trajectory of enhancement, although to retain sales at the bottom end of the market the company's cheapest models remained very basic, the smallest being only fourteen and a half inches long. With regard to dolls' houses, their wooden construction meant that they could be easily and cheaply modified even in mid-year, but by 1924 a new comprehensive range was available with small metal-framed windows. As was customary, prices catered for all pockets but the most elaborate models had so many extras that they were beyond all but the wealthiest of purchasers. The miniature wooden furniture for the houses was also available in a variety of traditional styles and Walter was always very proud of the fact that the firm was asked to make the furniture for a maid's bedroom in the specially commissioned dolls' house designed by Sir Edward Lutyens and presented to Queen Mary at the British Empire Exhibition in 1925.

Product innovation was also evident in the transport toys. Pull-along wooden models of London buses and the traders' delivery vans which were so commonplace on British streets were based on specifications provided by the manufacturers of the actual vehicles, while the ill-assorted collection of pull-along railway engines listed in 1919 was replaced by a new range in 1922. The following year saw the introduction of Puff-Puff engines, which, as the name suggests, emitted smoke by means of a mechanism patented by one Herbert Renton who took the idea to Lines. It was an immediate success, selling over 3,500 in its first full year. Another huge success was the Pedal Fairykar launched in 1924. Inspired by the success of the Fairycycle, Walter had designed a small version with the pedals placed through the front wheel as a way of encouraging younger children to learn to walk. It proved to be so popular that it was eventually made in folding form, and also in a safety version with a proper chair seat: there was even a Fairymotor, which simply housed the whole thing inside a model car body. The pedal cars themselves had already benefitted from qualitative improvements, first through the use of better-quality plywood for the bodies, and then by the introduction of tubular steel for the chassis which made the vehicles much lighter. Further refinements remedied the tendency of wheels to work loose and the introduction of machine-cut chain wheels helped reduce complaints that the drive chains disengaged too easily from their cogs. A further innovation abandoned the chain drive mechanism altogether in favour of a new double crank movement, first introduced in the Comet car in 1924. This new drive system was soon incorporated into all the cheaper cars and even some of the more expensive models. Eventually, too, features such as number plates, fascia, and speedometers became standard on all but the very cheapest models. Then, in 1926, there rolled off the production line a new model, the Lizzie, cleverly named after Henry Ford's original Tin Lizzie motor car, but significant mainly as a pointer to the future because it was the first all-steel pedal car to be made by Lines.

Constantly increasing output for both the home and overseas markets, realising new concepts, improving older ones and diversifying the basic materials and manufacturing processes, all required additional inputs or different combinations of both plant and labour. Nickel-plating machinery was installed in 1922, for example, along with new welding machines and additional polishing and tool-making plant.

One consequence was the company's increasing capitalisation, another the growth of the workforce which reached 400 by 1924. The existing Ormside works could not physically accommodate such expansion and additional facilities had been taken in the Old Kent Road, giving a total space of well over 100,000 square feet. In 1921, a separate office and a dedicated showroom had been opened in Moorgate, the nerve centre of the British toy trade and, as the location of many major wholesalers, a magnet for potential buyers. The opening of a showroom was yet another illustration of Lines Brothers' progressive approach, for as one trade journalist observed at the time, 'old methods of doing business can no longer be relied upon, and the firms who have moved with the times, and adjusted their sales policy to the changed conditions are reaping the benefit.'[35]

The risk, of course, was that piecemeal development would signpost a route to the same sort of haphazard physical expansion which had characterised G. & J.'s business, but it was made clear as early as the 1923 AGM that this would not be allowed to happen. A 700 per cent increase in the tonnage of turnover since 1919, it was reported, made it essential to concentrate production on one site with room for further expansion in the future. This would produce the economies and enhanced efficiency necessary to pay off the new capital required whilst also increasing turnover, profits and the return on shares. In fact, the brothers had already identified a suitable site at Merton on the outskirts of London. Twenty of the available forty-seven acres were purchased immediately along with a one-year option to buy the remainder. Inspired in part by a visit to Hornby's Meccano works in Liverpool and drawing on his previous efforts at factory design in 1914, Walter drew up the plans for the new plant. The merits of both the move and his design were set out in a cogent memo, presumably prepared for shareholders and headed simply 'Some of the reasons for the new factory'. It pointed out that a single site would reduce overheads by eliminating the carriage of goods between factories, while the office staff currently coordinating work between the different premises would be freed up to deal with the extra output rising from the move. Furthermore, the layout of the various departments relative to others could be improved. It went on to argue that there would be cost savings on artificial light because the proposed new factory would be a single-storey building with roof lights, and power would be generated from wood waste, much of which was currently given away. Insurance would be cheaper and access to the adjacent railway siding would save some of the money currently allocated to carriage costs. Finally, more space would be available for an improved packing, dispatch and finished goods store, as well as for any additional machinery needed for future innovations.[36]

It was a persuasive document, but once the building itself was completed it took six months to fit out the interiors. Almost a quarter of a mile in length, the factory comprised thirty separate departments dealing with a variety of manufacturing processes such as electroplating, stove enamelling, and metal presswork. The enamelling department housed seventeen stoves while the paint department with its six drying rooms was comparable, in the opinion of the editor of *Games and Toys*, with the only other one he had seen – which was in a car factory. Similarly, Lines' new nickel-plating plant was only the second such machine to be installed in Britain, the other one also being in a car factory. The editor noted, too, that finished toys for export were boxed with different coloured labels for each country. It was an altogether impressive operation and a major testimony to the brothers' logistical abilities that the entire plant was moved to Merton over a single weekend at the end of June 1925. The transition was well-publicised in an intensive advertising campaign which, as usual, went down particularly well with the trade press.

The move had several consequences. On the downside, the capital expenditure involved in equipping the new site was high and necessitated a temporary increase in the company's bank overdraft. At the AGM in 1926, Walter proposed to deal with this by increasing the company's nominal capitalisation to £200,000, a quarter of which was to be issued immediately with the rest held in reserve against future capital expenditures in order to minimise reliance on the banks. There were also some initial labour difficulties which Walter tried to gloss over. At least, when a statement was issued to customers in October 1926 warning that prompt delivery could be guaranteed for only a limited range of toys, the ostensible reason given was that order books were already full. But the more likely explanation was the need to recruit additional workers, some to support the projected increase in the scale of manufacturing, others to replace those who could not afford to travel to the new location. In the short term this may have had the effect of slowing output as the new employees learned the requisite processes. At all events, Lines' labour costs certainly increased, by £17,000 according to the chairman's report at the 1926 AGM, an expenditure which rather ate into that year's £27,000 increase in turnover. Soon, however, the number of employees at Merton reached 500, most of them enjoying not only relatively high wages but also the leisure opportunities provided by their employers. Some of the surplus land on the site was put down to tennis courts and football pitches, and facilities made available for other sports including boxing and athletics, while the company's regular social activities included various clubs, dances, and annual outings, usually to the south coast. There was little unique in such an approach since many large employers in Britain made similar provision, but combined with Arthur's sensitive handling of personnel affairs, for which he was primarily responsible, it probably helped to ensure that labour relations at Merton were generally good.

One more immediately positive outcome of the move was that advance preparation for the annual rush season became easier because there was now sufficient storage space for packed finished goods, and, as had been anticipated, it also proved easy enough to simplify office procedures. On the manufacturing side there was a massive rise in annual turnover which, as Table 2 indicates, reached more than half a million pounds by 1928–9, supported as always by significant increases in advertising expenditure, by £5,000 in 1927 alone. In part, this growth in turnover reflected the greater degree of self-sufficiency conferred by the expansion of manufacturing capacity. From 1927, for instance, Lines began to make its own wheels because there was now adequate room to install the requisite machinery – high-speed rollers to form rims and mudguards, machinery to fit tyres automatically, and special rollers and conveyors to move wheels between departments. By the end of the decade, all the various types of wheels required were being manufactured in-house. Reduced dependency on outside suppliers had obvious economic benefits and also reduced the risk of piracy, an important consideration since in the past a few less scrupulous external contractors had sometimes leaked details of Lines'

Table 2. Lines Brothers Ltd. Turnover and Profit 1925–1929

Year	Turnover (£)	Profit (£)
1926–7	471,686	31,440
1927–8	496,773	38,032
1928–9	531,004	38,734

Source: MOC. P. Lines Archive. Uncatalogued. Lines Brothers Ltd. Turnover and Profit. Typescript note.

new products in advance. Even more significantly, the heavy investment in additional plant that accompanied the company's relocation ensured that its productivity continued to exceed that of others in the sector: even before the move to Merton a Ministry of Labour survey showed that, in 1923, each Lines worker was making 625 prams a year compared with 458 at the other leading maker, Patterson Edwards.[37] The comparable figure for G. & J. was a paltry 181, which made something of a mockery of the poem which Joseph composed when his sons moved to Merton, warning them of the dangers of competition from G. & J. A further advantage of this higher productivity was that it allowed Lines to offer some of the cheapest prices on the market: their 25/- (£1.25) pedal car body, for instance, was considerably larger than the equivalent model offered by Patterson Edwards for 28/6d (£1.42 ½p).[38]

The most significant ramification of the move, however, was the opportunity it offered to shift from an old to a new medium of production. Timber had long been the major material used both for prams and toys. An official government report calculated that in 1918, wooden toys made up twenty-three per cent of total domestic production, compared with eighteen per cent for light metal, sixteen per cent for dolls, four per cent for prams, and three per cent for heavy metal, with the remainder a mix of items such as soft toys, lead soldiers and so on.[39] Virtually identical proportions were reported in another survey published in 1927, the only difference being that pram production was now included with the mixed group.[40] As far as Lines was concerned, the firm certainly introduced some of its best known wooden toys between 1927 and 1930, including the L B Motor, a tip lorry, a two-seater Rolls Royce, a fire engine, a Buick and a Rolls Eight. A new range of six Cotswold style dolls' houses appeared in 1928, designed by the company architect to a slightly smaller scale than earlier models and with a novel opening back. Lines' total output of wooden toys actually peaked in 1927 but the beginnings of a transition were already apparent. In that year's catalogue, four newly designed wooden dolls' prams appeared alongside five other new models of varying sizes but made of steel. The new material proved so successful that a year later only one of the listed dolls' prams was made of wood. Folding tubular steel pushchairs for babies were also in the 1928 list, although the conversion of baby prams took several years to complete. As for the smaller ranges of floor toys, a steel steam crane unveiled in 1927 proved so popular that by 1929 there were four different models to choose from: a year later four commercial vehicles based on a common steel chassis were also available. The first steel pedal car, the Lizzie, had been produced earlier in 1926, but at the 1927 AGM, Walter quoted a letter from an Australian agent complimenting the firm not only on the quality of its packaging but also on the use of steel instead of plywood for the bodywork of the Comet model.

Although he went on to point out that the use of steel was a development only then reaching a more complete stage, it was clear that its advantages as a manufacturing material would ensure its further utilisation. Steel did not warp or split, whereas wood was particularly prone to such failures, especially in the different climatic conditions of the numerous countries to which Lines was increasingly exporting. Steel construction also made it easier to manufacture detachable wheels, thereby allowing goods to be partially dismantled and thus more readily packed for transit. Finally, features such as beading and moulding, which on wooden items had to be added by hand, could be readily integrated into the pressed body of a metal pram or toy, reducing the requirement for skilled labour.

But if steel was becoming more prominent in Lines Brothers' products, from the second half of the 1920s onwards the necessary investment in the appropriate machinery created problems of its own. Historically, toy sales had always been very seasonal with demand concentrated in the months prior to Christmas. Like other manufacturers, Lines had usually responded to the troughs and peaks in demand by varying the size of its labour force over the course of a year, although the pram business afforded the firm some latitude in smoothing out this cycle. However, steel processing made the business more capital intensive and it made little economic sense to invest in plant and then leave it relatively idle for significant periods of time. One obvious response was to make goods in advance of the peak season and put them into stock: indeed that had been among the reasons advanced to justify the acquisition of more capacious premises at Merton. Yet such was the volume of increased output that it soon proved necessary to look for yet more space. As Walter also pointed out at the 1927 AGM, local storage facilities were expensive and for that reason, he went on, it had been decided to rent substantial premises in Oldham. Goods were to be loaded onto trains at Merton and carried to the new warehouse which was directly adjacent to a railway siding. Doing away with the packing and crating would save on freight charges, he said, and there would be additional saving on packaging materials. Company vans would then deliver to outlets within a fifty-mile radius around Manchester.

Oldham may have seemed an odd choice of location but it was a canny one. First, it gave the company a physical presence in a heavily populated region singularly short of toy manufacturers. Toy making had blossomed briefly in Liverpool under the artificial conditions of wartime but it shrivelled away once peace returned.[41] By 1927, and despite Meccano's presence, the north west was no longer officially recognised as a major toy-making centre, the region then possessing just forty-six of the 405 toy manufacturers extant in Britain, whereas 210 were based in or around London.[42] Second, Oldham was less than seven miles from Manchester, for decades the venue for the country's most significant toy trade fair. It is true that its importance had been somewhat diminished by the advent of the BIF, the opening by firms such as Lines of their own showrooms, and the increased deployment of travelling salesmen – but certainly not to the extent implied by one journalist who asked sardonically, 'What is Manchester Toy Week? A period of social activity designed to enrich hotel proprietors. What is Manchester? An industrial city in Lancashire, entirely surrounded by toy trade representatives.'[43] As far as Lines Brothers was concerned, however, the opening of the Oldham depot in August 1927 was followed by an increase in the firm's sales in the region, prompting the *Toy Trader* to comment that 'like an irresistible force, the progress and development of Messrs Lines Bros Ltd., goes on steadily from year to year.'[44]

Certainly when Walter presided at the AGM in 1929, he could look back with some pride on what had been achieved in the ten years since he and his brothers had launched their business In the space of a decade, the whole production side had been effectively transformed into a modern engineering operation. Turnover had multiplied to exceed half a million pounds, and profits had risen by eleven per cent. The dated and inconvenient Ormside works had been replaced by custom-built premises which, funded in part by a new share issue and the sale of some surplus land, were expanded again in 1929 to create a factory area of some 300,000 square feet. Another new factory was also being constructed in Handsworth for the Unique and Unity Cycle Company which by now was manufacturing all the firm's cycles and which, in the early months of 1929, had become the first of the many subsidiary businesses which Lines Brothers acquired. The only survivor among its original directors was the owner James Munn and in a pattern frequently to be replicated, Walter, Will and Arthur comprised the rest of the Unique and Unity board.[45] At Merton, several hundred well-rewarded and well-treated employees worked in modern facilities on advanced machines to produce an astonishing array of toys, increasingly in metal rather than wood, and from 1926 under the new brand name of Tri-ang. As with the abandoned 'Triangtois' label, Tri-ang was advertised as being synonymous with quality and value for money at the top and bottom ends of the market both in Britain and overseas.

Right from the start the company had sought to develop its foreign trade, but inflation and currency fluctuations had made this difficult in the immediate postwar years, while the government's decision to return to the gold standard in 1925 at the prewar level had overvalued sterling by about ten per cent, making British goods relatively expensive in international markets. Nevertheless, Walter and his brothers made a point of attending Europe's most important annual toy fair at Leipzig, and he was able to report in 1927 that Tri-ang toys were available throughout much of western Europe and Scandinavia, as well as all of the dominion countries, the Indian subcontinent, Argentina, Brazil, Chile, the United States, and China. It was indicative of their sensitivities to international buyers that from 1928 the catalogues and price lists began to include metric measurements.[46] In theory, the overvaluation of the pound in 1925 also made toy imports relatively cheap, but in fact the annual value of foreign toys entering Britain remained pretty even throughout the 1920s. In any case, Walter, despite his support for tariff protection, had unbounded confidence in Tri-ang, telling shareholders in 1928 that Lines Brothers had 'nothing to fear with any foreign competition and can cope quite well with anything that might arise in this direction.'[47]

The elements which had contributed to Lines' rapid and profitable development – investment in new production facilities large enough to exploit emerging technologies and materials, a stress on marketing and distribution both at home and abroad, together with continuous product innovation – are all among those identified by one leading scholar as the keys to business success in the period.[48] Yet, as was true of British manufacturing generally in this decade, expansion was not accompanied by any fundamental changes in the company's managerial organisation. Lines remained a prime example of 'personal' management whereby the directors effectively controlled most of the business themselves. Not only did they (together with their close family friends on the board) continue to hold most of the shares, but they involved themselves directly in the daily activities of the firm, exemplifying what has been called 'the golden age of directorial power'.[49] This was typified by Arthur's practice of patrolling the shop floor at Merton and also by Walter's continued and detailed scrutiny of the annual catalogues. Surviving draft copies are all heavily annotated with suggested descriptive glosses pencilled in by his hand. His proposed changes to the entry for Pedigree prams in the 1927–8 catalogue, for example, included specific reference to innovative features such as 'Dunlop tyres', 'uncrackable leather cloth – new innovation', and 'metal bodies, integral moulding'.[50]

Personally, too, the brothers were now beginning to benefit from their hard work. Both Walter and Arthur had married in the course of the decade and, like Will, were able to provide quite handsomely for their growing families. All three could afford a relatively luxurious lifestyle, including generous housing and, for their children, access to an enormous range of toys. What Walter described as the 'small remuneration' they had initially agreed to draw over the first few years had been augmented by £100 a year in 1926 but had always been more than amply supplemented by handsome returns on their shareholdings. Walter's own dividends amounted to slightly more than £4,347 after tax in 1927, and over £5,500 in each of the two succeeding years, just shy of £350,000 in today's values. Not only was he personally wealthy but he was clearly the best known of the trio, leading what had become in a remarkably short period of time one of Britain's largest and most diverse toy manufacturers. This had been recognised both by his peers in his election to the presidency of the industry's trade association, and also by officialdom when he was appointed in 1926 to the trade board, whose meetings he attended assiduously, and his membership of the BIF's advisory committee. In recognition of his achievements, and his standing, he was offered a CBE in the 1929 honours list. But Walter, whose numerous attributes certainly did not include excessive modesty, was not at all pleased. He thought his work merited a knighthood and he complained in no uncertain terms to his brother-in-law, James Rae, a high-ranking civil servant, who had some involvement in the honours process. Rae replied tactfully that he had described the offer to his colleagues as 'a bloody insult', adding 'I hope you won't think I have had anything to do with it. My connection with Honours is confined exclusively to those given for political services.'[51] This particular black cloud may have loomed darkly over Walter's personal horizon but far more dangerous was the storm which broke with frightening suddenness over his business when, at the end of October 1929, the Wall Street stock market in America collapsed.

Chapter Three

Rough Roads, 1929–45

The United States had emerged from the First World War as the world's dominant trading and lending nation and it was inevitable, therefore, that the collapse of its stock market would have international repercussions. As far as Britain was concerned, the ensuing global economic slump resulted in a downturn of industrial output, modest perhaps by comparison with the experiences of America and Germany, but at 11.4 per cent still significant. Second and consequentially, there was a sharp increase in unemployment which, according to the official count, reached 3,000,000 by 1932, although the actual figure was probably rather higher. Finally, the nation's balance of payments deteriorated as world trade contracted, causing British manufactured exports to decline by about a third, and also reducing income from invisible exports. A surplus of £104,000,000 in 1928 had, within three years, become a deficit of some £114,000,000. Against this background, European liquidity problems helped spark off a financial crisis in Britain over the summer of 1931.

America's own banking system proved remarkably frail in the aftermath of the Wall Street crash, with some 2,000 institutions failing. As American investors sought to protect themselves by withdrawing funds from Europe, the crisis of banking confidence spread. First Austria, then Germany, and finally Britain came under severe pressure. Gold and foreign currency began to trickle out of London and then threatened to become a torrent with the publication of the May Report at the end of July 1931, which suggested that the rising burden of unemployment relief was pushing Britain towards a massive budget deficit. Paralysed by this affront to the prevailing economic orthodoxy that national budgets should be kept in balance, Ramsay MacDonald's Labour Government first dithered, then divided and finally disappeared altogether to be replaced by a national administration pledged to stringent economies to restore the nation's financial credibility.

It was not surprising that in such circumstances demand for non-essentials such as toys stagnated; in the United States the leading trade journal *Playthings* contracted to a mere eighty pages from its previous 400. Protected as it was by a seventy per cent import tariff, the American toy market had never been an easy one for British makers to penetrate although firms such as Lines making high-end goods, or like William Britains with a niche product, had had some limited success. Now, however, other overseas markets began to shrink as governments everywhere sought to protect their own manufacturers by imposing tariffs. Britain's total toy exports fell continuously from 1929, plunging to an interwar low of some £378,000 in 1932. Domestically, rising levels of unemployment and a package of expenditure cuts, including reductions in public sector pay and the withdrawal of the government subsidy for the BIF, also weakened the demand for toys. The general gloom was reflected in the columns of the *Toy Trader* which, in the spring of 1930, described business as poor and the outlook uncertain, commented that there was no optimism at the Manchester trade fair and concluded that the toy trade was feeling the full force of the slump.[1] The mood at the fair was equally flat a year later, notwithstanding an appeal from the manufacturers' association to buy British toys at Christmas in order to boost employment.[2] Inevitably, businesses began to struggle and of some 2,460 toy enterprises extant in 1930, only 1,330 were still functioning by 1940.[3] The casualties included leading merchant houses and importers, such as Wisbeys, Bedington Liddiatt & Co, and Whyte, Ridsdale and Co. Nor were manufacturers immune, and among the best-known names to fold were Multum in Parvo, founded in 1896, and the Liverpool firm of Gray and Nicholls. Bassett-Lowke's wage bill fell by ten per cent as it laid off workers, profits at both Meccano and Britains shrank while Reka survived only by abandoning toys altogether. As for Lines Brothers, figures for the year ending September 1932 showed a small fall in pre-tax profit of about five and a half per cent. (Table 3). According to Walter's son Graeme, this so depressed him that he considered offering the entire Tri-ang operation as a going concern

Table 3. Lines Brothers Ltd. Annual Pre-tax Profit 1930–1940

Year	Net pre-tax profit (£)
1930–1	44,207
1931–2	41,730
1932–3	44,435
1933–4	61,689
1934–5	61,774
1935–6	68,406
1936–7	79,717

Source: The Times, 30 June 1936

to Frank Hornby.[4] Unlikely as this may seem, a similar claim was also made by E. R. Robinson, the managing director of Meccano's French subsidiary at the time, and the suggestion gains added credibility from at least one intriguing document in the surviving Meccano archive, a note from Meccano's advertising manager to the Daimler motor company dated October 1934. It is typed on paper carrying a printed heading containing the address of Meccano's Liverpool factory, but the company name appears as 'Meccano Tri-ang Limited', indicating perhaps that Meccano executives had even begun to draft appropriate stationery which they then subsequently used up when the proposal failed to materialise. Yet it seems highly unlikely that Walter's heart was ever really in the idea, and it was perhaps prompted by what was little more than a marginal decline in the annual profit.[5] His, after all, was a pretty irrepressible personality and any pessimism was probably little more than a passing whim, more feasibly perhaps brought on by the fact that the most prominent toy firm of all to go down during the slump was G. & J. Although there was often confusion in the public mind between the original firm and Lines Brothers Ltd., the sons were pretty much cut off from their father, at least in commercial terms. They had sold back their G. & J. shares at par when they set up on their own, and while they still occasionally supplied the old family business with parts, Joseph had continued to make his own distinctive playthings throughout the 1920s. But by 1930 he was well into his eighties and his toys, too, had aged, appearing rather dated in style. His firm's output and asset value were both very low, he did not exhibit at the BIF in January 1931 and at the end of the year he died. He was justly heralded as the grand old man of British toy making, but he was never fully reconciled with his three independently minded sons: none of them were beneficiaries of the £33,543 he left in his will. G. & J. was wound up, Lines Brothers bought the assets and George, who had gone to work with his father in the mid-1920s after finding it difficult to make his farming pay, finally joined his siblings, albeit as an employee.

Another notable victim of the slump was Britain's most prestigious toy shop, Hamleys, which went into liquidation in 1931 with gross liabilities of more than £159,000. Its origins went back to the mid-eighteenth century but it had been in trouble for a number of years, never really recovering from a huge overshoot on the estimated cost of rebuilding its Regent Street premises and an ill-fated satellite development at Eastbourne. Catering primarily for the well-to-do (the sales floors were all carpeted), Hamleys' management had signally failed to move with the times. Profits in 1928 were a pitiful £302 and the slump perhaps made customers, who were predominantly account holders, reluctant to settle outstanding bills on time. In 1930, trading losses of over £4,600 were incurred and although this did not deter the directors from paying a dividend, a second year of poor results brought the receivers in. It was, the *Toy Trader* remarked, 'the biggest set back the toy trade has been called upon to face for many years.'[6] Set back it may have been, but for Walter Lines it represented an opportunity. According to his son, Walter believed that the best response to economic hardship and uncertainty was to exude confidence, preferably – as he put it – by the chairman going out and purchasing another Rolls Royce.[7] Perhaps it was in this spirit that in 1932, the very year when profits dipped, Lines Brothers' official letter heads began to contain the claim that the company was the largest toy manufacturer in the world. In fact, in terms of employees it was not at that time even the largest toy company in Britain, since evidence presented to a government inquiry at the start of the year suggested that Chad Valley had a considerably larger workforce.[8] But Walter's apparent flippancy about the chairman's mode of transport masked his intuitive understanding that the best time to invest and innovate is in the depths of a slump. He also had a certain sentimental attachment to Hamleys, dating perhaps from his boyhood when he had delivered G. & J. toys to the store or possibly from his construction – for £30 – of the bespoke dolls' house which Edward Hamley had provided for the Queen of Spain. More pragmatically, Lines Brothers was Hamleys' most significant manufacturing creditor, owed about £890, although the toy and fancy goods dealers Eckhardt was due over £1,300. Furthermore, Walter could see the potential of Hamleys as a showcase for Tri-ang products, not least because the international reputation of the store ensured that its catalogues circulated widely. (For similar reasons when, as chairman of Lines Brothers, he was later offered the royal warrant as a supplier of toys and sports goods to the Queen, he asked if it could be transferred to him as chairman of Hamleys because he knew that far more people would see the royal coat of arms displayed at the shop than at the Merton factory.) However, he was acutely aware that the purchase of the country's best-known toy outlet by its leading toy maker carried a risk of alienating the trade more widely, so before completing the purchase he prudently checked that other manufacturers would continue to supply Hamleys.

Appropriately reassured, the Lines Board paid out £32,000 for the retailer's assets, debts, and properties, including numbers 200 and 202 Regent Street, which were held on lease from the Crown on a fixed, low-interest mortgage of £80,000.[9] Walter later wrote that when Hamleys was acquired 'a good many things needed putting right', but he was confident that profitability could be restored by improving the management and injecting larger cash resources.[10] He also felt that there was scope for a thriftier approach to purchasing and the newly appointed general manager R. W. Dullam was instructed to buy economically, irrespective of the supplier. Dullam himself confirmed years later that 'pulling a sinking business together in 8 months was, shall I say, "difficult"!'[11] The difficulties included his discovery that some of the staff were fiddling the books and the fact that Walter, with his usual energy, insisted on immediate changes to the layout of the building, compelling the unfortunate Dullam to work (and in fact sleep as he stayed overnight) in what was effectively a building site. The fourth floor, previously used for storage, was modernised and converted into a selling area ultimately given over almost entirely to Tri-ang products. Further space was released by shifting the offices from the third floor to the back street while the packing and dispatch departments, two floors below ground level, were entirely refitted with steel racks instead of wooden ones, and equipped with a mechanical conveyor as well as a new franking machine. The additional cash to which Walter had referred became available when Lines formed a completely new subsidiary, Hamley Brothers Ltd., capitalised at £50,000, made up of 45,000 cumulative preference shares of £1 and 100,000 ordinary shares at 1/- (5p) each. The parent company's interests in the new enterprise were strongly entrenched in the structure of the rejigged Hamleys' board whose eleven members included not only the three brothers, but their sisters Winifred and Mary, together with their fellow Lines director George Campbell and sales manager George Inglis.

The process of turning this new business round was a demanding one because its financial position was dire. In the eight weeks between Lines' acquisition of Hamleys and the incorporation of the new company there was a net loss of almost £3,800. A small profit was returned on sales of £14,785 between 8 October and 26 November 1931 when the receiver finally handed the business over to Lines Brothers' control. Over the following three months to the end of February 1932, which covered the Christmas season, sales rocketed to £45,424, although the net profit was still small at £824. The analysis of costs as a percentage of sales, itemised in Table 4 below, gives a clear idea of the steps taken to turn the business round. Thus, the reduction in interest payments reflected the injection of new capital resources and the immediate paying down of the mortgage, while the huge upsurge in advertising and catalogue expenditure was predictable, given Lines Brothers' own strong belief in the value of publicity. Because the Regent Street premises occupied Crown land, no reductions could be secured in their ground rent, rates or taxes, although savings under these headings were achieved by the prompt closure of other Hamley outlets. But it took time for the benefits of these measures to work their way through into the balance sheet. With no dividend declared in 1934, Walter reckoned that if payments

Table 4. Hamley Brothers. Costs as a Percentage of Sales

Item	8 Oct–26 Nov 1931	27 Nov 1931–29 Feb 1932
Wages and salaries	4.93	6.18
Interest	4.7	2.76
Advertising	1.78	6.97
Catalogues	1.25	3.53
Carriage	4.26	2.88
Rent	3.53	2.29
Rates	2.80	1.74

Source. MOC. P. Lines Archive. Uncatalogued. Hamley Brothers. Trading and Profit and Loss Accounts as at 29 February 1932

on the ordinary shares were possible within three years of the Lines' takeover then the shareholders would be happy.[12] His optimism was justified, for the position improved consistently thereafter. A small profit in the year ending February 1935 had climbed by 1937 to £7,460, progress which the chairman modestly described as satisfactory.[13] The improvement might conceivably have been even more marked had Dullam not been headhunted by Gamages after eighteen months or so. What Hamleys lost by his resignation was well-captured in Walter's reference to his 'hard work, loyalty, strict integrity, and adaptiveness'.[14] It was some time before an adequate replacement was found, which may explain why questions were raised at subsequent annual meetings about the sales staff's poor treatment of customers and continuing problems with the rendition and settlement of accounts.

It was typical of Walter Lines, and the personal style of capitalism his business typified, that he responded to these concerns by saying that he would look into them. He was as good as his word, for later reports mentioned considerable improvements in staff behaviour and performance. That he even found the time to investigate such apparently trivial matters was quite remarkable, given the wider challenges facing him at Hamleys, not to mention his ongoing activities as a major spokesman for the whole industry, and from 1936 an additional representative role as president of the Regent Street Association.

In another sense it was remarkable that Lines even took Hamleys on when it did, for there were signs that intensifying competition in the domestic market was causing some concern in the Tri-ang boardroom. It is true that the directors never remotely entertained a proposal that Tri-ang toys should be made redeemable against special toy tokens put into cigarette packs by tobacco manufacturers, but there were other revealing straws in the wind. A letter of April 1930, for instance, informed the firm's travellers that the company's traditional policy of maintaining retail prices on products was being abandoned with respect to the new Rover junior model car. With a wholesale price of 13/- (65p) each or 12/- (60p) for a bulk order of thirty-six and no maintained (fixed) retail price, the intention was clear enough – to 'upset any competition on the cheaper range'.[15] The same document also asked for responses to the idea that competition in London should be countered by abandoning maintained prices for certain other pedal cars. The replies do not survive but must have been positive: by 1931 Lines had six new little models on the market, all bearing the Tri-ang label but with no maintained price. One consequence of this new approach seems to have been the disappearance of the Lizzie, up to that time the firm's cheapest and in some ways its iconic model. A few months later, another circular went to retailers and representatives announcing a new modified version of the Pedal Fairykar, again designed to compete with a cheap rival product marketed by Leon Rees.[16] In similar vein, a scrawled note in an anonymous hand and headed 'Catalogue 1930-3' commented that with respect to items such as miniature golf greens and pedal cars 'we find considerable competition because some of our cheap toys are maintained & comps. are not.'[17]

If competition in the home market was intensifying, international prospects were equally difficult, even more so after the Australian government raised its tariffs on British goods from thirty to forty-five per cent. Faced with the likelihood of declining sales in what had hitherto been a tough but generally receptive outlet for their products Lines Brothers sought additional overseas markets. Walter, spurred on by a government initiative to promote trade with Argentina, went off to attend the 1931 British Empire Trade Exhibition in Buenos Aires with every intention of securing a foothold in that country. He reached a preliminary agreement with the firm of Casa Gesell, offering a down payment for the goodwill and exclusive use of the name, with the intention of subsequently buying the company's factory and other assets. The total cost of the deal was some Argentinian $738,000, at the prevailing exchange rate the equivalent of slightly more than £118,000. Walter returned to England to put the plan to his board, promising a decision by the end of February 1932. In the event, however, the Argentinian company apparently backed out. 'I suppose you know,' runs an unsigned and undated note in the Peggy Lines archive,

> that we came to an agreement to buy out Casa Gesell but they backed out at the last minute. I was very sorry because even tho' conditions appear to have got worse I'm sure they're a sound business. We've appointed new agents and are hopeful of doing modest business through them .... I feel sure that we shall eventually carry out what I cannot do, even if it means establishing our own factory.[18]

From Lines Brothers' perspective the Ottawa Agreement, concluded in the summer of 1932 and establishing arrangements for a system of imperial preference, represented an additional obstacle to overseas business. In theory, signatories agreed to give preference to exports from other territories within the British Empire, but this proviso did not always benefit toy manufacturers. Thus, when Australia removed its duties on British goods, toys remained subject to a sixty-one per cent tax because they were classed as luxury goods. Walter told guests at the trade association's annual dinner in 1936 of his strong conviction that the most favoured nation clauses in the Ottawa arrangements had also had an adverse effect on trade.[19] In particular, the American market, already heavily protected, had been made even more inaccessible because, under the Ottawa Agreement, any reduction in the tariff on British goods would also require the Americans to make the same concession for every other country in the world (except Germany with whom there was no commercial treaty). Free trade, Walter told one correspondent in 1932, was what the world needed.[20] His apparent change of stance from his position in the early 1920s was short-lived, however, for a few years later he was once again urging that the trade should be protected from overseas toys produced in cheap labour economies.[21]

The worst effects of the depression lingered in Britain for the rest of the decade in the form of the high unemployment, which blighted the nation's staple industries in the north, south Wales and western Scotland. Other economic measures, however, pointed to recovery as early as 1933, its causes variously ascribed to the government's abandonment of the gold standard in 1931, which allowed sterling to find a more realistic exchange value, the introduction of a general twenty per cent import tariff in 1932, the reduction in bank rate, or a fortuitous shift in the terms of trade which reduced the cost of imported food and freed up consumer spending power. The effect of these changes on the trading environment for toy manufacturers was mixed. The 1932 public expenditure cuts probably helped to dampen domestic demand, whereas leaving the gold standard was welcomed by the industry as cheapening exports, raising the cost of imports, and benefitting those manufacturers using mainly domestically sourced raw materials.[22] Tariffs were seen as similarly beneficial and overall toy imports certainly fell sharply from £2,191,000 in 1930 to £892,000 in 1932. *Games and Toys* was particularly jubilant in reporting that the price of German imports would rise to the benefit of domestic producers.[23] But the downside of tariffs was a modest increase in domestic competition, especially as some foreign toy makers responded by setting up businesses within the UK, a trend that accelerated as Nazi persecution drove a number of German Jewish toymen to flee their own country. Some indigenous manufacturers also gained additional protection against foreign goods from an order which came into effect after some lobbying by trade associations in October 1932, and required all toys costing more than 2d (slightly under 1p) to be marked with the country of origin or simply as 'foreign'. Although as president of the trade association Walter Lines had led a deputation on this matter to the Board of Trade in March 1930, Lines Brothers itself did not provide evidence to the inquiry, probably taking the view that the Tri-ang brand was well enough established in the public mind.

The import duty on toys, initially set at twenty-five per cent, was reduced to ten per cent in the summer of 1933 very suddenly and with no prior consultation, but this did not seem to dent the renewed optimism already apparent in the British trade. *The Times* claimed that the 1933 Christmas season was the best in living memory for British-made toys, and the Manchester fair the following February certainly saw an upturn in the number both of exhibitors and new products.[24] Business at that year's BIF was described as 'good' and Walter certainly seemed to be in cheerful mood at Tri-ang's AGM later in the year.[25] The company's export efforts had started to bear fruit, he said, because markets which had been practically cut off for the past three years were beginning to open up again. After the blip of 1932 things were also brightening up on the domestic market, and it was with some obvious satisfaction that Walter reported Lines Brothers' highest profits to date. This upward trajectory continued for the rest of the decade with turnover reaching a million pounds by 1940 and profits rising steadily. The momentum was generated by a successful combination of traditional toys and a flow of new ones so constant that a catalogue listing 109 items when Lines Brothers moved to Merton in 1925 grew by 1939 to contain more than 500.

To some extent, of course, the firm was protected from the worst effects of the slump both by the sheer scale of its operations and the geographical spread of its markets, as well as by the fact that while children, however reluctantly, might sometimes have to be deprived of luxuries such as toys in times of hardship, babies still needed prams and specialised furniture. Lines certainly did not allow the economic downturn to interfere with its programme of continuous improvement in pram design, hence a note to dealers in January 1931 announcing that recently introduced detachable ballbearing wheels had proved so popular that they were being incorporated into many models as a standard feature, while motor-pattern tread jointless tyres were adding to the prams' visual appeal. Concurrent improvements to pushchairs included the introduction of cast hubs and ribbed cushion tyres on the wheels, while in 1932 Lines branched out further into the lucrative infant market by launching a completely new range of nursery furniture. Making cots, high chairs and playpens had an added economic rationale in that it utilised the firm's woodworking capacities at a time when metal was progressively replacing timber in several of its other traditional lines. There was even an agreement to mark Lines' toys and nursery furniture with the logo of Mickey Mouse or other Disney characters, but although Walt Disney Mickey Mouse Ltd. had similar arrangements with almost two dozen other British firms, its relationship with Tri-ang did not run altogether smoothly. Walter found the Americans' obsession with legal detail frustrating. Complaining about their tardiness in agreeing the final terms of the licensing contract, he commented rather sharply that 'we know very well lawyers love to put in all sorts of things and are normally the source of nine-tenths of the difficulties.'[26] In the end, Lines designed only a small number of items specifically for this scheme, the bulk being drawn from existing products, but within a couple of years many of them had been returned to the ranges for which they had originally been intended, even though some still carried the Disney imagery.

Other initiatives with wood were, however, more successful. Having catered for infants' comfort, it was a logical step to provide for their learning needs as well and the Tri-ang Teach'em Toys for 3 to 5 year olds appeared in 1937. This range of educational toys included Tappit sets and bricks, together with existing climbing frames and playhouses. To encourage sales, Will instructed his salesmen to target all the nursery schools, hospitals and pre-school bodies in their areas, and to visit local directors of education. In the same vein, and the same year, Lines also produced Fit-Bits, a patented construction toy in which wooden parts were connected by means of rubber tubing, although in commercial terms the toy probably did not meet the high expectations with which it was launched. Conversely, the brightly painted wooden pull-along Toddler Toys which followed in 1938 did so well that by 1940 they had been augmented by three further ranges offering greater play value in the form of sound generated by bells, and greater animation provided by the use of eccentric or cranked wheels

Concurrent with the diversification into nursery furniture was a range of sailing yachts, providing yet more work for the woodworking departments. None of the initial eight models proved very successful, however, because the sheer size of the solid wooden hulls and the weighted keels required to deliver a satisfactory sailing performance made the boats liable to capsize and sink. A fortuitous solution appeared in 1933 when the company was approached by George Kellner, who had been making toy boats in Germany using a patented resin body fastened to a wooden deck. Effectively, this allowed the weight of a thirty-inch boat to be reduced by more than two-thirds. Early in 1934 it was announced that Lines had acquired exclusive rights to manufacture and distribute 'K' boats, Kellner having also been taken on to run a newly established boat department.[27] The first yachts made to the new specifications appeared quite quickly, but the process itself was costly and within a year or two they had been joined by a number of smaller and simpler vessels with pressed steel hulls and aimed at the cheaper end of the market. Kellner left in disgust when his trademark 'K' was put on these items, but by 1940 Tri-ang was making more than forty different types of boat. In a significant pointer to the future, one of them was made by using injection-moulded plastic.

These timber-based ventures into corners of the market previously untapped by Lines Brothers certainly served as a useful supplement, albeit with varying degrees of profitability, to the firm's existing ranges of traditional wooden toys. The rocking horses, for example, survived, though now sometimes in more simplified form with flat, cut out heads instead of carved ones. A new series of dolls' houses, marketed as 'Attractive houses at affordable prices' and designed by Ken Barrington-Smith, the company architect, did so well that Smith followed up with three, more expensive, Tudor-style houses resembling those then being built in increasing numbers in the London suburbs. By 1933 there were twenty-nine different houses in the Tri-ang catalogue, but after that the only major innovations consisted of some flat-roofed models reflecting contemporary house design, and then a sudden flurry of cheaper models just before the war.

Although such timber goods still made up a significant and diverse proportion of Lines Brothers' toys, in the 1930s steel was becoming ever more common, particularly for larger items. The Tri-ang stand at the 1931 BIF, for example, displayed a range of vans, lorries, and cranes, all items which previously had been made in wood but which were now turned out in metal, and advertised as showing the free hand of the engineer rather than the carpenter in their design and manufacture. A similar change was taking place with respect to dolls' prams so that by 1936 only four of the twenty-six available models were still made mainly from wood, with the most expensive of all barely distinguishable from their full-size Pedigree equivalents. As for the company's best-known product, the 1930–31 catalogue still contained thirty-one pedal cars with wooden bodies, but twenty-two of the twenty-nine models in production four years later had pressed steel bodies. The first metal car had appeared as early as 1926, but the transition accelerated after 1929 when steel radiators based on American Chevrolet and Buick automobiles were added to existing wooden-bodied cars. Although metal could be pressed to incorporate the detailed features which in wooden models had to be added by hand, thereby reducing the need for skilled woodworkers, the initial tooling costs were much higher and metal work required labour with different skills. This meant that the most efficient manufacturing approach was to produce a single basic car body, which could then be differentiated by the addition of varied radiators, wheels and other components. Despite the economies of scale which this offered, Lines continued to offer numerous additional features on its most expensive top models, a legacy perhaps of the old days but not one which optimised economic efficiency.

At the opposite end of the scale, possibly in response to government pleas to reduce imports and encouraged by the fact that Bing Brothers, the major German maker of clockwork and tin toys, was in difficulty, Lines also started to develop a new range of small mechanical toys. It took some time to tool up and the necessary plant required additional factory space but the first models, featuring a push-and-go movement, appeared in 1931. Tri-ang's clockwork models followed in the catalogue for 1932–3 and proved more appealing to customers even though the initial range of tanks and tractors was rather underpowered and did not perform as well as the publicity boasted. Nor could they have added much to the profit line, for the board insisted that they be retailed at 6d (2½p) which, given the prevailing mark up in the trade, meant they were sold to distributors at three quarters of that. Nevertheless,

Walter told the 1932 AGM that he hoped to have thirty different models available for the next Christmas period and the range survived into the 1940 catalogue, as did a follow-up series of clockwork vehicles made up at Merton using pre-printed bodies brought in from another firm.

By far the most successful product of this type was undoubtedly the Minic range, first introduced in the 1935 catalogue and effectively the first clockwork model that was recognisably a Lines Brothers' concept rather than a copy of other products. Made to a consistent scale, and plugging the gap between the large-scale models already available and the highly successful diecast Dinky toys recently launched by Meccano, Minics went very well with the O gauge model train sets still very much in vogue. From a manufacturing point of view, they had the great advantage that one type of motor could be installed in any model, and of the first fourteen vehicles made only six required separate tooling, the rest sharing a standard body and chassis. Purchasers were encouraged to become collectors by the inclusion of a dedicated catalogue in each box, and sets offering several different vehicles together, or allowing a child to build a model from its constituent parts, were also made available. Over the decade the number of Minic models increased greatly, their play value further enhanced by the addition of special toy garages and a service station. They were hugely popular, with total sales at Hamleys alone in 1935 reaching 11,418 units by 12 December, 'with the best two weeks of the year to go'.[28] Volume manufacture ensured that notwithstanding their relative cheapness and small margins, they contributed consistently to Tri-ang's profitability.

Some of the smaller parts for Minics – ladders for fire engines or exhaust pipes for racing cars for example – were made of plastic supplied by International Model Aircraft (IMA), an associate company which Walter later claimed as a Lines Brothers initiative.[29] In so doing, however, he rather glossed over IMA's earlier antecedents. Model aeroplanes had appeared almost as soon as the first real flying machines on which they were based, although both were equally primitive in appearance and performance. The First World War served as a powerful catalyst for the development of flight, and in the course of the 1920s, two Kentish brothers, Charles and John Wilmot, both of whom had served in the

Royal Air Force, and Joe Mansour, a modeller from Lancashire, started to work quite independently on improving model aircraft. Unaware of each other's work, their patent applications were submitted at virtually the same time but after the Wilmots read about Mansour in a letter he published early in 1930 the three men finally met. Eight months later, Wilmot, Mansour and Company, capitalised at £100, appeared in a list of newly registered companies listed by *Flight Magazine* for 29 August 1930.[30] The company's FROG trademark, conventionally thought to stand for 'Flies Right off the Ground', was logged the following March, and then in December 1931 the name of IMA Ltd. was formally registered.[31] In February 1932, the new company exhibited its first product at the BIF, a 1/32 scale flying model called the FROG Interceptor. The fuselage was made of thin duralumin sheet, the wings and tail of pre-printed card, with the wings and undercarriage fitted in such a way that they detached when the plane landed and could be easily refitted. Its most innovative feature, however, was a winder built into the box which, combined with a gearbox in the plane's nose, meant that the propeller could be more in scale, and the plane could fly for longer than other existing models. At this point, and well aware that they lacked the necessary financial resources to undertake volume manufacture at a consistently high quality, Wilmot and Mansour made an approach to Lines Brothers. It is conceivable that this was influenced by the fact that Mansour had worked on the Queen Mary dolls' house to which Lines had also contributed, although it seems far more likely that financial considerations were the main driver. Even though interest rates in 1932 were at their lowest for thirty-five years, leading to cheap mortgages and a consequential surge in house building, to which some scholars attribute economic recovery, the banks still remained cautious when it came to industrial investment, commonly charging five or six per cent on business loans. In that environment it was hardly surprising that small businesses or individuals with new ideas should seek alternative sources of funding from established manufacturers: as the country's leading toy maker, Lines Brothers was an obvious choice.

Although Walter Lines was himself a gifted and innovative toy maker, he was always open to other people's ideas, once telling James

Rae that he was 'of course interested in anything which is really novel, which is in our line and which can be turned into a saleable product on a decent scale.'³² In this spirit, for example, the firm had responded to a contemporary craze for miniature golf, which swept the country in 1930, tempting not only several newcomers, but also well-established firms, including Tri-ang, to produce their own versions, in the process exhausting just about every known synonym for the word 'miniature'. However, when Walter learned about the FROG plane, possibly at the BIF when it made its debut, he knew a good concept when he saw one. Popular interest in flying had been stirred by recent British success in the Schneider Trophy races and the Lines board responded favourably to IMA's approach, agreeing to provide premises, capital, and tooling in return for the IMA patents. Charles Wilmot and Mansour were taken on as IMA's salaried joint managing directors, initially for seven years. Such was the level of Lines' investment that, by November, it was claimed, 800 Interceptors a day were being made.³³ That Christmas saw mass press advertisements for the plane, and Hamleys even had the models flying around its front foyer.

Walter made much of IMA's progress over its first year and anticipated a successful future for it. However, tooling up for further models would require specialist machinery, adding to the similar need already generated by the diversification into mechanical toys and the increasing use of standard pressed steel bodies in pedal cars. Yet additional equipment needed space, already under pressure from the expansion of the wooden toy ranges and the establishment of the new boat department. Furthermore, to be utilised most efficiently, machinery needed to be run on a regular basis, resulting in continuous streams of product which then had to be stored against advance orders, whether actual or anticipated, creating yet more demand for space. The question for Lines, therefore, was how to fund the new plant and extra space, and then to support ongoing development with additional working capital, given that the seasonal nature of the trade had, at times, driven the company's overdraft as high as £90,000, which incurred relatively high interest charges. In outlining this situation to shareholders, Walter pointed out that while property could be funded by long-term mortgages which were comparatively inexpensive, thanks to the government's cheap money policy, the banks were still prone to charging much higher rates of interest on shorter term loans for industrial expansion, as IMA had discovered. Furthermore, the likely amount of expenditure needed made it unrealistic to look to existing shareholders, already numbering fifty, the legal maximum allowable for any private company. The solution, as recommended by the board, was that the firm's private status be abandoned and the shares made available to outside investors.[34]

The formal announcement followed in 1933 to the effect that in order to finance a £50,000 factory extension and the purchase of new equipment, Lines Brothers was to become a public company. The move was not totally risk free. Among financial experts there was a general wariness about industrial investment following a series of spectacular failures during a share boom in 1928 and then the arrest for fraud of C. C. Hatry, one of the period's most prominent industrial financiers. In fact, it was further testimony to Lines' commercial success, and reputation, that the 200,000 new £1 first preference shares issued at five and a half per cent were taken up very quickly, raising the firm's capital resource to some £400,000. G. F. R. Baguley, an accountant, now joined the board to represent the first preference shareholders. The necessary changes in the original Articles of Association also required the three brothers to abandon their status as life directors. Each then accepted a formal seven-year contract as joint managing director. The arrangement whereby Walter and Will alternated annually as chairman was also ended, with Walter becoming chairman at an annual salary of £2,400 plus his director's fees and remuneration. A further effect of the change was that the brothers lost their priority rights to buy any shares which became available, and the other existing shareholders also forfeited their rights to buy any such shares which the brothers did not take up. The board's previous powers to approve the sale (and the price) of shares to outsiders also disappeared. Walter slipped rather glibly over these potentially tricky implications at the extraordinary meeting called to discuss the issue of going public – he for one had no intention of allowing the changes to weaken his family's control of the business.

Lines' first ever public share issue proved so appealing that by the summer of 1934 part of the proceeds had already been successfully converted into bricks and mortar, a new factory for IMA on the Merton site. The following year Lines acquired the remaining shares in IMA, which became a wholly owned subsidiary. The early success of the FROG Interceptor naturally encouraged the development of further models and concepts, most notably, from 1936, the Penguin series of construction kit scale models made in cellulose acetate, a material which allowed for the incorporation of greater detail than was possible in the wooden modelling kits then commonly available. Nearly all the Penguins had moving parts such as propellers, wheels and retractable undercarriages, which increased their appeal but tended to make them expensive. By mid-1938 there were sixteen models in the range, and Imperial Airways (a forerunner of the British Overseas Airways Corporation) even commissioned 1,000 models of its flagship aircraft, the four-engined Empire flying boat, for publicity purposes. Lines approved this deal, partly because Imperial was paying but mainly because it provided a major publicity opportunity for IMA. More generally though, the Penguins were not particularly profitable because moulding cellulose acetate was a slow process which drove up unit costs, the packaging was expensive, and customers soon discovered that some of their lovingly constructed models had a tendency to warp or degrade. Nevertheless, IMA's turnover was high enough to support about 180 workers by 1939. Profits, however, were relatively low and do not seem to have benefitted the parent company very much. Walter's daughter Peggy Lines, who spent some time as a school teacher before joining the family business in the 1960s, later suggested that Mansour and Wilmot might have kept a tighter control over their finances, while Arthur Lines was pointed in his reply when the pair asked for a salary increase in 1938.[35] He agreed to a rise of a pound a week, but stressed that while Lines' investment in IMA was very large, it had seen little return on it and had not shared in the profits accruing to IMA. After expressing concern that IMA's overhead costs were still rising, he concluded quite bluntly: 'The Directors of Lines Bros Ltd do a good deal for you in the course of the year in way of work and advice and we consider that it should be possible, in the future, for your Company to pay something for this assistance.'[36] Even so, and despite these signs of disquiet at senior level, involvement with IMA did provide Lines with capacity in what would be the next major medium for toy manufacture, and even before war broke out in 1939, IMA's plastics expertise was being utilised in other product ranges, including Minics, boats and dolls.

The development of IMA under Lines' tutelage was a further manifestation of Tri-ang's astonishing expansion in the course of the 1930s, which necessitated the opening in January 1935 of a new London showroom in Union Street, three times larger than the company's original premises in the capital. Another was the continued growth of the workforce which reached 2,500 by 1936, making Lines one of the largest firms of any sort in the country at a time when only 649 out of the nation's 173,500 manufacturing enterprises employed more than 1,000 people.[37] Business historians have suggested that in other major industrial economies such levels of growth were accompanied by major organisational change within individual businesses.[38] The consensus is that in interwar Britain, however, this did not happen to any significant extent, a conclusion largely borne out in the case of Lines. It is true that the firm's expansion required the sourcing of additional, outside capital, hence the decision to become a public company. Yet this certainly did not result in any significant separation between ownership and control, for the brothers and their relatives still retained the bulk of the equity and comprised the majority on the board. Similarly, the use of a subsidiary company model, a common feature of the wider merger movement occurring in Britain at the time, ensured that control of the various new business acquired over the decade was kept firmly in the parent company's hands. It is perhaps worth noting that none of these acquisitions appear to have come about as part of any deliberate strategy: in most cases – K boats, FROG, and what became Pedigree – the initial approach was made *to* rather than *by* Lines. Hamleys was the only purchase actually initiated by the company and even then there is no evidence that Lines would have moved to buy it, had it remained viable in its own right.

Further confirmation that, despite its growth, Lines had not moved beyond the personal capitalism stage of development is provided by the persistence of the brothers' extensive supervision over its operations, well captured in Arthur's case by his nephew's later description of him as the company's 'i dotter and t crosser'.[39] Some idea of the detailed scrutiny Will exercised over administrative matters can be gleaned from one surviving but undated document requiring the anonymous recipient to investigate at least once every week the state of the packing and dispatch department, order typing, general typing, the sales and purchase records, all ledgers, queries and complaints, time-keeping records, wages department files, railway accounts, 'plus any more you can think of'. The outcomes were to be recorded on cards, kept confidential and handed in monthly to the directors.[40] His standards were equally demanding when it came to shop-floor processes, and his brusque notes must sometimes have made uncomfortable reading for the recipients. Typical was one, which went to the head of the pram fitters' department, with reference to customer concerns that brackets on prams had been working loose because the fixing screws had not been properly burred over. It ended with the thinly veiled threat that 'I trust we shall not have this complaint arise again.'[41] A similarly admonitory note was dispatched to the woodwork shop when buyers pointed out that cots were prone to collapse because the pins intended to hold dowels in place were often inserted incorrectly.[42] He was equally terse when a failure to meet some delivery dates in 1934 forfeited a good deal of customer goodwill. He promptly appointed two chasers whose task was to report daily to the directors and identify any delay in the processing of orders. 'We trust all foremen will see to it that they are not responsible for any delay.' After pointing out that no article should take longer than four days to go through the factory from manufacture to dispatch, he added that in his opinion 'a really properly rushed order could be got through in one day complete, including all painting and drying.'[43] He was equally forceful with senior members of staff, completely overruling sales manager George Inglis when he resisted a proposal that the firm make a quality pram to retail at about £15 rather than the £10 which was the firm's current upper limit for its cheaper ranges.[44]

Walter, too, remained closely involved in the minutiae of the business and was equally hard-nosed. Years later he referred to the five-minute tea and toilet breaks which had become common during the war as 'bad habits . . . refinements' serving no useful purpose 'except to reduce the amount of work done'.[45] He could, however, be constructive as evidenced by his neatly pencilled comments and suggestions in surviving company catalogues. Similarly, when the company architect presented his draft plans for the Tri-ang stand at the 1936 BIF, Walter went into considerable detail about the changes he wanted, even to the extent of specifying the size and placement of the cutout plywood letters on the stand, and suggesting that the new carpet have leaded ends to avoid any need to nail it down.[46] Above all, his boardroom involvement never quenched his basic aptitude and passion for designing and constructing toys. In 1931, a salesman hoping to get a large order from Marks & Spencer told him about a rival company's dolls' pram on sale in Winchester for 5/9d (roughly 29p), which was lower than the cheapest priced Tri-ang pram. Walter himself promptly set to and engineered a cheaper model to sell to the trade at 3/9d (slightly less than 19p) each. He knew that it would affect sales of Lines' own cheapest pram, which was larger and much better quality than its rival, but was confident that his new model would 'knock out all opposition'.[47] It did. In similar vein, a note of January 1936 asked his brother George, working in the technical department, to consider a number of very specific product difficulties but also offered a number of possible solutions. A complaint that on one clockwork model the spring was not strong enough for the heavy body could, he suggested, be addressed by reducing the gear ratio so that the car ran for a shorter distance for each winding: on some of the pedal cars he wanted changes made to switches and fittings to avoid problems with the lights, and proposed further refinements to the body colour, the bonnet profile, and to the rather dated wings.[48] A few months later he was writing to another draftsman because he wanted to design a new radiator for the ordinary standard Minic saloon and improve its mudguards and lamps. He added that he would like to make similar changes to the Vauxhall model and his engineering expertise was evident when he laid out the various process options by which bright plated flutes could be added to the model's bonnet.[49]

Shortly after Walter wrote this letter, the Lines board went to the stock market again to raise yet more capital (see Table 5). Just before the offer closed, 390,000 of the 5/- (25p) ordinary shares, credited as fully paid up by way of capitalisation of undistributed profits and reserves, were given to the holders of the original 50,000 1/- (5p) shares in proportion to each individual's holdings. Arthur, Walter, and Will had themselves already derived a more than comfortable return from their shareholdings – the six-month dividend payable on the ordinary and preference shares in July 1931, for example, had earned Walter slightly more than £5,350 after tax, well over £350,000 in today's terms – but the new proposals represented a handsome windfall for those who had invested right from the start.[50] Walter and Will each promptly sold 40,000 and Arthur 20,000 of their allocations at 21/- (£1.05) per share to the underwriters, Erlangers, who also purchased another 100,000 on the same terms. Erlangers then put the whole 200,000 onto the stock market at 22/6d (£1.12½p) each. Noting that Lines Brothers was the largest business of its kind in Britain and that its profit curve had dipped

Table 5. Lines Brothers Ltd. Issued Capital 1920–1935

Year	Capitalisation (£)
1920	36,087
1921	39,556
1922	43,081
1923	46,363
1924	72,387
1925	100,000
1926	100,000
1927	129,510
1928	136,210
1929	151,210
1930	156,710
1931	157,710
1932	169,685
1933	400,000
1934	400,000
1935	400,000

Source: *The Times*, 30 June 1936

only three times since 1919, the *Financial Times* gave the shares a strong recommendation to would-be investors looking for future high yields.[51]

In his letter to Erlangers proposing the issue of the new shares, Walter had indicated that some £45,000 of the proposed new capital would be set aside for the purchase of land and plant. His apparent reluctance to be more specific perhaps reflected a certain amount of embarrassment, because it soon transpired that the land in question was five acres of the original plot at Merton that had been sold off in 1929, although Lines was now also hoping to get the buildings and plant left by a series of unsuccessful proprietors. The reason for the acquisition soon became apparent when the new site was occupied by Pedigree Soft Toys, another wholly owned Lines Brothers subsidiary, incorporated as a private company in June 1936. In line with their usual practice, the brothers all became registered directors with Will as chairman. They were joined on the board by other company stalwarts, Inglis and Baguley. All five were allocated a single £1 share with the rest of the £10,000 capital held by Lines Brothers Ltd.[52] As with IMA, the original impetus behind this initiative was external, coming from a small group of animal artists seeking financial support. Conscious perhaps that one brand new soft toy manufacturer, Merrythought, had enjoyed remarkable success since its establishment as recently as 1930, Walter leapt at the opportunity for yet another diversification, buying the operation together with its skilled workers and giving it a name with which Lines had, through its prams, been long associated.

Given their enduring popularity with children, it was predictable that teddy bears – no fewer than twenty-three versions ranging in price from 3/4d (about 16½p) to 20/8d (about £1.03) – should comprise the first Pedigree toy range. First year profits were small at just over £554, but the potential was considerable and the bears were soon joined by dogs, then ponies and horses, many in push-along versions with handles and wheels provided by Tri-ang's metal workers. Production of Pedigree dolls began in 1938, manufactured according to a patented process which, once again, Lines purchased from an inventor who was then employed to oversee the operation. A mixture of wood flour and resin was used to make heads and limbs, the filled moulds then being placed on the end of long poles which were held manually in a furnace. After being thus fired for some time, an arduous process which earned for the doll department the unenviable soubriquet of 'Dante's inferno' from its operatives, the parts were painted. It was not a particularly efficient process because as the moulds cooled so bodies and heads tended to fracture, while the paint was also prone to cracking: nevertheless, the method was used to make all but one of the 243 varieties of Pedigree doll available by 1940.

Processing problems, whether at Pedigree or IMA, were not the only difficulty Lines was encountering as the 1930s drew to a close. International relations both in Europe and the Far East had been steadily deteriorating for some years to the point that British governments eventually felt it necessary to embark on a programme of rearmament. Inevitably this pushed up the demand for, and thus the cost of, steel. In 1937, the Iron and Steel Federation (ISF) agreed that its affiliates would standardise the price of their output. Toy manufacturers protested so vigorously when one company was refused a pre-ordered supply of steel unless it paid the new standard price, that the ISF actually repudiated the action of its own member. Walter complained to *The Times* in November that the ISF's stance was effectively barring Britain from world markets and making it very difficult for firms trying to export goods made with British steel.[53] But his letter ended with a rather lame denunciation that the policy was absurd and someone should stop it. Although he was writing in his capacity as chair of the trade association he clearly had more than a vested interest, for Tri-ang itself was clearly feeling the pinch. A note to dealers in May 1937 blamed recent price increases for prams and folders on the rising cost of steel.[54] His annoyance was still simmering at the following year's AGM when he referred to the 'outrageous steel prices' which had cost his company sales, especially of those exported goods in which steel was the main component. Mindful perhaps that his remarks might alarm shareholders, he hastened to add that Tri-ang's continued success was certain because as far as possible they were finding substitute materials.[55] His confidence was backed by an announcement that a thirty per cent dividend would be paid for the third consecutive year.

Within a year, however, Britain was once more embroiled in world war and the country was shifting onto a war footing. Walter was on a family holiday in Skye when Prime Minister Neville Chamberlain announced the commencement of hostilities with Germany and he immediately motored back to his Surrey home to oversee the shift of production priorities which would inevitably ensue. Less than a fortnight later he told a meeting of the trade board that toy manufacturers in general were already finding it difficult to obtain basics such as timber and screws, and he proposed that representations be made to the Ministry of Supply. The following month he went into print to announce that his company was taking on no new customers because its transport had been requisitioned, the price of raw materials, when they were available, was escalating, and like all other businesses Lines Brothers had been required to insure its stock.[56] Some idea of the red tape which rapidly engulfed the company can be gleaned from a circular issued by Pedigree at the start of September, explaining that it was withdrawing its current price list immediately, raising the price of existing orders by ten per cent and all new orders by double that. Although the increases were attributed in part to higher wages brought about by the need to fund paid holidays under recent legislation, and the latest pay award agreed by the trade board, they were blamed mainly on the sudden cancellation of contracts by raw material suppliers, the legal requirement to insure all stocks, and the expenditure incurred on Air Raid Precautions (ARP) equipment and protective concrete trenches.[57]

Privately, however, Walter seemed to have been more accepting of these additional burdens on his business, telling his brother-in-law in December 1939 that while the war had brought some little worries, Lines' toy turnover was so far being maintained.[58] Indeed, during the early months of the so-called phony war, IMA's aeroplanes enjoyed a surge of popularity, and in November 1939 the firm's travellers were advised that both made-up and kit-form models of the Hampden bomber and a German Messerschmitt would be in production the following month. Another positive from Walter's point of view was the government's encouragement to raise export volumes in order to help finance the war effort, with Lord Forres, a member of the Export Council, going so far as to claim that 'every case of toys for export is another nail in Germany's coffin'.[59] In response, the *Toy Trader* incorporated into its title the words '*and*

Exporter' while *The Times* observed that 'toy making has a new dignity . . . it is an essential industry.'[60] On this basis Walter, leading a delegation to the Board of Trade earlier in the year, had been able to secure for toy makers an allocation of raw material equivalent to four-fifths of what they had used in 1938. Lines itself was certainly doing its best as far as exports were concerned, the *Illustrated London News* reporting in August that the company had doubled its overseas sales over the previous year.[61]

Two weeks later the war landed, quite literally, on Lines Brothers' own doorstep when half a dozen small bombs dropped in the course of a daylight air raid hit the Merton factory. The explosions smashed large parts of the roof, damaging in particular the main gas meter and high voltage transformer. It was now that the precautions about which Walter had previously grumbled proved their worth, for the exposed parts of the factory were immediately covered with tarpaulins, collected as already planned from the local ARP centre, and the necessary repairs were effected promptly. Walter made relatively light of the incident at that year's AGM, preferring instead to return to his favourite themes – the bureaucratic burden of form-filling connected with limitations of supplies, materials rationing, price controls, the new purchase tax and other returns required by various government departments. He also explained that with staff departing to join the armed forces and customers bringing their orders forward from the traditional August-December period, production schedules were under pressure.[62]

By the end of the year, however, and with Britain's military situation appearing ever more precarious, government economic policy was focused on sheer survival and toy manufacturing became ever more difficult. New emergency regulations were introduced, allowing firms to manufacture only with materials not considered essential for the war effort (effectively certain timbers and materials already in stock). Production of models in the Penguin range ceased entirely in 1941, and despite IMA's optimistic announcements of November 1939 very few new planes actually appeared thereafter. In the course of 1940, some kits were being packaged with notes explaining that particular items were no longer available because skilled toolmakers were increasingly occupied on war work, as indeed was the greater part of the factory.[63]

In fact, as Walter personally told one customer in 1943, Lines made no new toys from scratch after 1940, although under the government's Utility scheme, which allowed the manufacture of certain items deemed essential, a limited production of basic prams continued in one half of the north factory at Merton.[64]

But in the rest of the plant toy making had long been supplanted by war work, for as Walter pointed out to his brother-in-law in December 1939, 'the fact is we are really engineers', a point he emphasised by reference to Lines' employment of almost 3,000 workers (including the Unique and Unity factory) and its own chemist, its special metal-testing department and its self-sufficiency in electrical work. As one of the largest such firms in the country, Lines Brothers' assets were effectively and quickly absorbed into the national war effort, with Walter proudly telling Rae that one major aircraft manufacturer had been astonished by the rapidity with which Lines had turned out machine tools of the highest quality. Yet it was not always an easy co-operation. Walter's own business success had birthed in him a profound scepticism with respect to the ability of civil servants to handle economic affairs, which may explain his impatience with the spate of controls and regulations involved in the transition to a war economy. He was himself, he opined somewhat misguidedly, 'a fairly modest fellow but I do think that if they had made me Minister of Supply I could have done the job a jolly sight better than it is being done now.'[65]

It was a typically immodest claim on Walter's part, but there can be no doubting either the magnitude of Lines Brothers' development since its establishment, or the part it proceeded to play in the national struggle. When the official secrecy ban was finally lifted at the end of the war, it was revealed that the company's contribution included 12,000,000 land mines, thousands of metal target gliders, scale models of the Normandy coast to assist with planning the D Day invasion of 1944, and 1,000,000 Sten guns together with 10,000,000 magazines.[66] These statistics concealed Walter's own personal effort, because when Lines was first asked to manufacture the mark II version of the Sten gun, he redesigned it to eliminate its tendency to jam and discharge spontaneously. The company's output would have been even more impressive had not production been interrupted in the early part of

Table 6. Lines Brothers Ltd. Profit 1940–1945

Year Ending	Net Trading Profit (£)	Net profit post-tax (£)	Dividend on 5/- shares (%)
30 June 1940	110,456		30
30 June 1941	125,407	64,056	30
30 June 1942		70,613	30
30 June 1943		70,800	30
30 June 1944	119,015	49,297	30
30 June 1945	145,336	51,679	40

Sources: *Financial Times*, 19 December 1941, 13 January 1943, 30 November 1945: *Toy Trader and Exporter*, February 1944, p. 32, January 1945, p. 60, December 1945, p. 68

1944 when, during a night-time raid, a 1,000kg bomb hit the wood mill, destroying a specialist plywood press used for making laminated spars for gliders, leaving a crater twenty feet across and five feet deep, and starting three fires, although these were quickly extinguished. Some minor damage caused by flying debris was repaired within a fortnight, during which time the plywood press was also replaced. Nevertheless, some loss of production resulted, in the case of mine crates a drop of almost sixty-nine per cent, although that particular contract was tailing off anyway. Other products were more seriously impacted. Prior to the bomb, Lines had turned out thirty-nine pairs of glider wings a week, but now only twenty-eight were possible.[67] Initially, the damage completely halted the output of magazines for Oerlikon anti-aircraft guns, and while production was swiftly moved to a different part of the factory it was so reduced that a third of the female workers on that line had to be laid off.[68] The bomb damage doubtless helps explain the downturn in both trading and net profit evident for the financial year ending in June 1944, as set out in Table 6. But while taxation and other war-related costs still ate deeply into profitability the following year, the upward trend in trade was evident and the board, looking to the future with some optimism, felt justified in raising the dividend for shareholders.

Chapter Four

The Highway, 1945–1961

The successful Allied invasion of Europe in June 1944 marked the decisive stage in the course of the war, although it took another year or so before Germany was forced into unconditional surrender. But if the munitions produced at Merton were still needed, Walter, in particular, had for some time been anticipating reversion to normal peacetime activity. Six months before D Day he had approached J. K. Peppercorn, controller of factory and storage space at the Ministry of Supply, asking for details of premises which might be available either immediately or after the war.[1] In March 1944, he applied formally for Lines Brothers to be added to the list of applicants for accommodation, indicating in reply to the standard ministerial circular encouraging industrial development in depressed areas that he was interested in south Wales. He subsequently explained that he wanted between 300,000 and 400,000 square feet of space to meet existing and anticipated demand for the towed anti-aircraft practice targets which Lines was making from Newport steel. His longer term aspiration emerged when he added that a new factory in Wales would free up space at Merton for peacetime production and that steel toys could also be made in Wales.[2] Already, as he told a trade board meeting in October, he had so many foreign orders in hand for toys that he fully expected to be able to retain all the women currently working at Merton on war production, a claim he reiterated at the AGM in December.[3]

Certainly, he could look forward to a sellers' market. For one thing, the level of Britain's financial indebtedness by 1945 was such that exports would have to be prioritised in order to earn the dollars essential to sustaining and reconstructing an exhausted economy. Unlikely as it may have seemed, toy making was officially identified as an industry with the potential to contribute to this effort. All the world's main toy-producing nations had been directly involved in the war, and the development elsewhere of any substitute indigenous manufacturing capacity was too immature to represent a genuine threat to established manufacturers such as Lines Brothers. With the exception of Louis Marx, the American toymen remained largely insular in outlook, snugly complacent behind the high tariffs protecting their extensive and prosperous home market. Nor was there much prospect of immediate competition from either Japan or Germany, whose respective infrastructures had been so devastated by defeat that toy making was never going to be an immediate priority. Two years after the war's end, for example, only a third of Nuremburg's thirty or so makers had resumed production, and Walter was probably well aware of the parlous state of the German industry since his brother George was advising the British Intelligence Services sub-committee charged with investigating it.[4] Even by 1949 the German toys on show at the Leipzig Toy Fair were still generally judged to be crude and not competitive with British goods at all.[5] As for the domestic British market, victory raised popular expectations and sentiment if nothing else suggested that children, largely deprived of new commercial toys for six years, would be among the first beneficiaries of peace. Official thinking certainly appeared to be working on these lines because the quota on domestic toy production was being eased even before the war ended. At the start of 1944, the maximum allowable toy output was set at an eighth of the total production achieved in 1939–40. By August 1946, the proportion had been raised to two-thirds, and two years later the Limitation of Supplies Order was ended entirely as far as games and toys were concerned.

This latter was, however, a rather empty gesture, described by one leading manufacturer as 'silly and meaningless' because many other official constraints remained in place, particularly with respect to raw materials, prices, taxation and business freedoms.[6] Given the prioritisation of exports and the need to protect the value of sterling, as well as to replace housing and other physical assets destroyed during the war, the continuation of such controls was inevitable, even before the election in 1945 of a Labour Government with an inherent ideological commitment to a more centralised economy, and an ambitious programme of social reform and industrial reconstruction.

Predictably, Walter viewed all state intervention as an encumbrance on business, warning that the resumption of toy production was dependent upon manufacturers being allowed to acquire the necessary resources and being freed from restraints such as controlled prices and purchase tax. This, at least, was the line taken in the first report issued by the British Toy Manufacturers Association (BTMA), reconstituted in 1944 largely at Walter's prompting and providing him, as president, with a convenient platform from which to vent his frustrations.[7]

The chairman's concerns notwithstanding, Lines Brothers used the rather unlikely outlet of the personal columns of *The Times* in the run up to Christmas 1945 to announce that limited supplies of its toys would soon be available, and in fact the main factories were in full production within six months of the war's end.[8] Such was the level of pent-up demand, both at home and abroad, that even years later Walter completely lost control of his metaphors, describing it as an 'almost bottomless pit' so 'ravenous' that it swamped the traditional Christmas season and jammed the dispatch area at Merton with customers seeking to circumvent the strict rationing the firm was forced to impose.[9] The board was so confident that at the very first postwar AGM in December 1945 the dividend on the ordinary 5/- (25p) shares, which had been set at thirty per cent in every year since 1936, was raised to forty per cent. Output picked up so rapidly that almost as soon as the first postwar catalogue was issued in 1947 a supplement was needed. Perhaps it was in anticipation of just such a scenario that the board had earlier decided that the sales policies of the three subsidiaries – the Unique and Unity Cycle Company, Pedigree, and IMA – should be centrally determined and controlled by the parent company although otherwise they were to continue operating as autonomous organisations.

With demand so high, facilities were inevitably stretched, all the more so because Walter had intimated that the company wished to upgrade its design and research capabilities, a project which, in turn, would necessitate further outlays on buildings and equipment.[10] After six years of war the Merton site was certainly quite run down. Its air raid shelters were still stuffed with the munitions tools which the Ministry of Supply insisted be retained for twenty years, the football field was cluttered with debris and there was not even any paint available to cover over the buildings' wartime camouflage. However, hopes of further expansion at Merton were dashed by an official refusal, providing fresh impetus for the effort to find an alternative location. South Wales may have seemed an unlikely choice, but chronic unemployment in the region's coal and steel industries had led to its designation in the 1930s as a special area and, as Walter had discovered when discussing the matter with the Board of Trade in 1944, manufacturers were still being offered incentives to set up in the area. Among the several toy firms to take advantage of these inducements was Mettoy, which moved to Swansea during the war, to be followed subsequently by Louis Marx, Chiltern Toys, Poplar Plastics and Crescent. After extensive haggling over terms, and some reserve on the part of civil servants concerned lest Lines Brothers fail to secure an anticipated extension of its government contract for the supply of towed targets, Walter accepted the offer of the old Rotax factory at Cyfarthfa in Merthyr Tydfil. In his usual blunt fashion he made it clear that he was 'resentful at the treatment he had received from the Board of Trade and felt that his firm should have been allocated space.'[11] Four months later he was complaining that he had still received no details as to the terms of the lease or the likely rent, delays which he emphasised were 'in no way due to ourselves'.[12] His mood was not improved when officials started to remove plant from the factory, including some which Lines had intended to retain. 'It was very difficult to get any satisfaction in these matters,' was Walter's comment, surprisingly mild but still sufficient to galvanise the civil servants into raising the matter directly with the minister himself.[13] This was not as surprising as it might at first glance appear. As one of the country's largest businesses, Lines Brothers' engineering plant and expertise had contributed significantly to the war effort and it continued for several years afterwards to undertake contract work for the Ministry of Defence.[14] As company chairman and president of the trade association, Walter himself had some official standing. He also carried considerable personal clout, for if his impatience with civil service procedures and his sometimes less than tactful language occasionally ruffled official feathers, his achievements and his business acumen were widely recognised: tangibly so in 1945 when he was appointed first to

Joseph and Jane Lines with their family in 1893. One-year-old Arthur is sitting on his mother's lap and Winifred on her father's. Will Lines stands in the centre between his parents, while George is on the end of the group next to the cap-wearing Walter. Mary, the Lines' middle daughter, is just behind her father's left shoulder (*Courtesy: A. Lowth*)

The labour intensive and messy nature of rocking horse manufacturing is very apparent in this picture of G. & J. workers in the later nineteenth century. (*Courtesy: A. Lowth*)

This splendid model of a locomotive and carriage was produced by G. & J. to mark the coronation of Edward VII in 1901. (*Courtesy: A. Lowth*)

The Hatcham works in 1919, where it all began. (*Courtesy: A. Lowth*)

The Lizzie, Lines' first steel-bodied pedal car. (*Courtesy: A. Lowth*)

The first Minic range as illustrated in the 1935–36 catalogue. (*Courtesy: A. Lowth*)

A Minic dustcart. The author was given such a model as a birthday present in the 1940s.

The FROG Interceptor.
(*Courtesy: P. van Lune*)

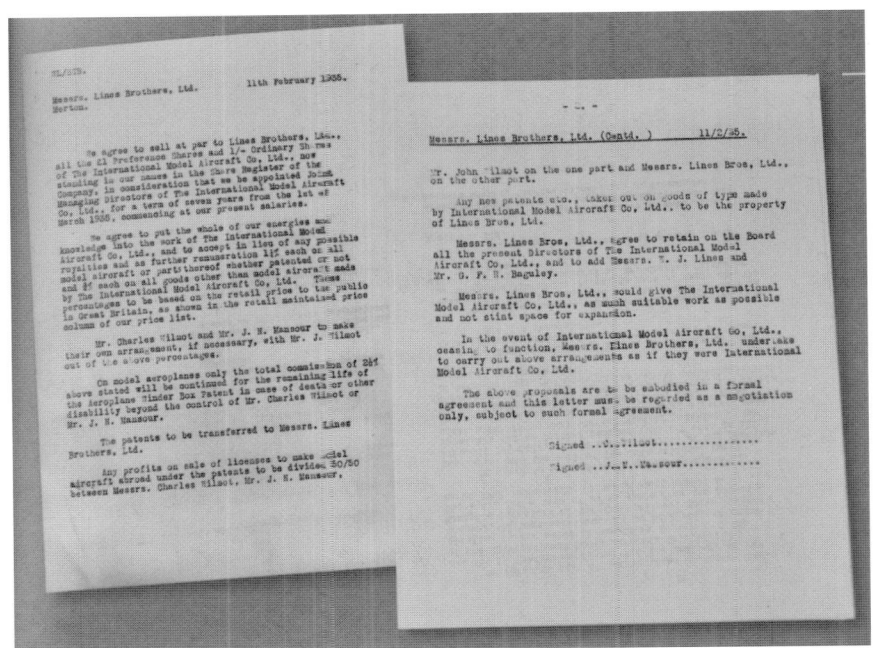

Draft terms of the arrangements by which Lines acquired IMA in 1935.
(*Courtesy: P. van Lune*)

The influence of the contemporary Art Deco movement is clearly evident in this 1930s Tri-ang dolls' house, a marked contrast to the more traditional Tudor style also available.
(*Courtesy: Wallis & Wallis Toys and Model Auctioneers*)

A Tri-ang mangle set from the 1930s, typical of the many small items produced for use in dolls' houses.

Section of the pram finishing shop c. 1937. (*Courtesy: A. Lowth*)

Advertisement from the 1941 *Games and Toys* trade directory, illustrating the extent of Lines Brothers' business since its establishment in 1918.

The Merton factory in the 1950s, justifying perhaps Lines' claim to be the world's largest toy-making concern.

Index to a 1950s catalogue, showing the vast range of toys and prams then being manufactured by Lines Brothers.

The inclusion of a card bearing the Tri-ang logo indicates that this Scalextric racing car set was manufactured very soon after Lines acquired Minimodels and before any significant development of the product had been undertaken by the new owners. (*Courtesy: Jon Mountfort*)

Spot-On diecast vehicles, Lines' late entry into what was a very competitive sector of the toy market in the 1950s. Their consistent scale and detailed modelling certainly enhanced their aesthetic appeal but also made the range comparatively expensive.

Arthur Lines in later life.

Will Lines in later life.

The changing of the guard. Walter Lines (left) was succeeded as managing director in 1961 by his son, Moray (right). (*Courtesy: P. van Lune*)

Leaflet announcing the merger of the Tri-ang and Hornby railway systems, following Lines Brothers' purchase of Meccano, makers of the Hornby range. This takeover was widely thought to have contributed to Lines' subsequent problems. (*Courtesy: Essential Works*)

Sindy and boyfriend Paul in 1965. The extended commercial success of these dolls was not enough to save Lines from collapse.

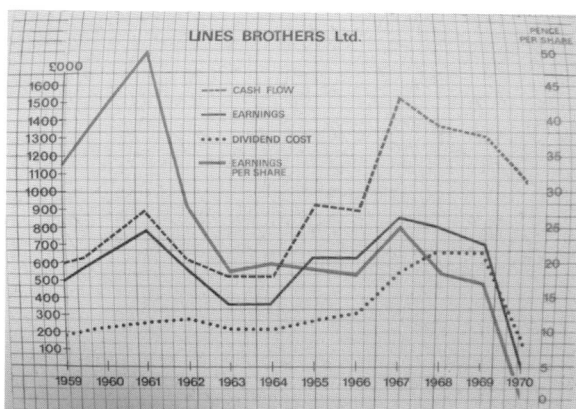

Graph showing the rapid decline of the Lines empire after 1966. (*Source: Review of the British Toy Industry, 1970*)

the Ramsden Committee charged with considering the future of the BIF and how fairs and exhibitions might be used to encourage exports, and then to the London and South East Regional Board for Industry.

The outcome of the minister's involvement in this particular spat over the Cyfarthfa plant was a high-level directive allowing Lines' managers to examine and retain such machinery as they wanted. There then ensued a protracted discussion over terms, before Walter beat the annual rent down from the £7,850 initially proposed to £6,500. In January 1946, the Treasury approved the Board of Trade's estimate for the factory's alterations in line with Tri-ang's requirements, the final cost eventually coming in at almost £86,000, considerably more than the £37,000 initially approved.[15] Delays in completing the factory's fitting out, not all of them attributable this time to the civil service, meant that it was early 1947 before production could actually begin, but as a related incident makes clear Walter, for all his grumbling, held by far the stronger hand in these negotiations with officialdom. Advised by his doctor to take things easy and not to drive, he had been provided by the company with a luxury car. When he applied to the regional petroleum officer for an additional fuel allowance to facilitate his frequent visits to supervise developments at Cyfarthfa, he was told that a much smaller vehicle should suffice. The company appealed directly to the ministry, which duly obliged on the grounds that the new Lines factory in south Wales was so important to the local economy. Lines Brothers (South Wales) was formally registered in September 1946.

In the same month, Lines Brothers (Ireland) was also registered. As in south Wales, the economy of Northern Ireland was heavily dependent on staple industries whose long-term viability was by no means certain, and local politicians were eager to diversify. That Lines might open a factory in Belfast was an idea first mooted with Walter by Westminster civil servants in June 1945, and he had taken it up with the Stormont Government. For his part, the Northern Ireland minister of commerce was much attracted by a proposition which promised within a year to bring a new industry and over 400 new jobs to Belfast, 130 of them for men.[16] Accordingly, the terms were very favourable, with Lines being offered not only a factory but also funding for machinery, together with extra supplies of controlled raw materials, especially steel.[17] Additional finance for plant, both in Belfast and Cyfarthfa, was raised from a new share issue.

From Lines Brothers' perspective, one attraction of setting up these regional factories was the cheaper cost and ready availability of suitable labour. But the greatest incentive was undoubtedly the official promise of priority in the allocation of raw materials, the scarcity and continued control of which provided constant targets for Walter's critical tongue through the early postwar years. As early as December 1945 he told the AGM that the firm's progress was being hindered, not only by officialdom's refusal to allow rebuilding at Merton but also by government restrictions on some raw material imports.[18] He was still pursuing this theme two years later, grumbling that his company's commitment to the export drive was being hampered by shortages of imported raw material needed for both manufacturing and packaging.[19] Both the Treasury and the Board of Trade, he told shareholders at the 1947 AGM, could be more helpful as regards import controls over raw materials. 'A company of our standing,' he added sententiously, 'is hardly likely to wish to import such things unnecessarily. The conditions laid down are arbitrary in the extreme.'[20] At the AGM in 1949, it was reported that the price of all the company's raw materials had tripled since 1938, and that currently the most pressing shortage was of thinner gauge steel. Scarcity was a recurrent theme in Walter's litany of postwar complaints, for Lines Brothers had to compete for supplies, especially of steel, with other high-demand sectors such as construction, shipbuilding, automobiles and armaments. Even so, the firm did not actually do too badly, securing on average some forty-five per cent of the toy industry's total steel allocation, although there could be significant short-term fluctuations.[21] The start of the three-year Korean War in 1950, for example, so distorted the market that shortages of steel, brass and zinc forced Lines to lay off 200 workers at Merthyr.[22] Walter led the complaints when the industry's steel allocation for the second quarter of 1953 was cut from 4,500 tons to 3,400 tons. With his own company's share reduced from 2,061 tons to 1,550 tons, he promptly put in a letter asking for an additional 250 tons, again warning that without it he would not be able to fulfil his export orders.[23] Of course it was possible to find alternative materials – Pedigree, for example, was using cotton waste instead of plush in some of its soft toys – but one possible substitute for steel, aluminum, was not always suitable and was, in any case, more expensive (as indeed was cotton waste compared with plush). As for plastic, Lines was certainly extending its use but it was not always a viable substitute for metal and, in any case, the company's plastic toys did not contribute significantly to vital dollar-earning exports since Canadian and American manufacturers were already using more advanced machinery and had a much greater capacity for plastic toy production. Deputising for his brother at the 1951 AGM, Arthur Lines attributed that year's low increase in trading profit partly to the restrictions on the supply of sheet steel, which meant that significant dollar export orders had had to be turned down.[24] In the same year, a consumer report prepared by the Board of Trade noted that there were still notable shortages in the shops of toys such as cycles, dolls' prams and pedal cars which were made primarily from tubular steel.[25]

But whatever the limits on Lines' ability to acquire the amount of metal it wanted, at least there *was* a domestic steel industry to which it could turn. It was a very different situation with regard to timber, still a major component of many Tri-ang toys but the bulk of which had to be imported. The Board of Trade's 1951 survey commented also on the fact that the production of large wooden toys was being inhibited by raw material shortages, with Lines Brothers singled out for being 'particularly behind with their deliveries'.[26] It was in the hope of alleviating some of the risk of timber shortages that almost as soon as the war ended Lines acquired W. Pearce, a business specialising in indigenous woods. It was, however, too small an operation to provide anything like the amount of material required by its new owners who remained heavily dependent on imports, the volume of which was centrally determined by the timber control body. The imported wood was then divided by a materials committee of the cabinet between the various ministries, each of which issued licenses allowing individual firms to purchase a stated amount – if they could find it. Alternatively, distribution between firms was entrusted by the ministry to trade bodies such as the BTMA, with the ministry holding back a portion for non-affiliated firms. In the prevailing economic environment the system was quite defensible, but the actual quantity of wood imported at any particular time inevitably fluctuated according to the level of international demand and changes in the purchasing power of sterling, which in the immediate postwar years was volatile. Any reduction in the total amount of timber imported meant reduced allocations to ministries so that, for example, the Board of Trade was allotted 600 stands of softwood in the second quarter of 1946 but only about 150 in the fourth quarter of 1947. For that same period the plywood allocation was more than seventy per cent down on what it had been in 1946, and that of hardwood, the most important for toy makers, was just over 10,000 cubic feet as against 200,000 cubic feet in 1946. The system ensured that these reductions eventually worked their way down on a pro rata basis to individual firms, but sudden fluctuations on this scale in the supply of a key raw material made production planning very uncertain. Walter, in particular, seemed to have had little sympathy for the difficulties facing a government trying to revitalise an exhausted economy at a time when the demand for everything always threatened to outstrip the supply of anything. As always, he appealed to the government's own priorities, pointing out at a meeting with the Board of Trade in 1947 that the export of wooden toys was low because the industry was being allocated inferior quality timber. It had little effect, for in November 1947, Lines Brothers was protesting strongly about the plywood allocation to Merton, while its Irish subsidiary told the BTMA that it was 'appalled' when its application for thirty stands of softwood, 15,000 square feet of hardwood, and 60,000 square feet of plywood resulted in allocations of nine stands, 950 and 17,000 square feet respectively. Trading on his previous dealings with civil servants, Walter was never averse to trying shortcuts by applying directly to the Board of Trade for additional supplies. As a civil service memo dated 19 July 1946 noted, 'this firm seems to have a habit of forwarding applications here which we pass to group without comment.' He was still at it six years later, applying in May 1953 for a supplementary supply of softwood.[27]

Lines' impatience with official red tape also extended to the export sector. Desperate to increase overseas earnings, especially of dollars, the government set ambitious sales targets for the toy industry. With overseas orders accumulating even before the war ended, Walter made it clear at the 1945 AGM that while the firm was fully committed to supporting this effort, it was impeded both by the shortage of materials and the bureaucracy attached to exporting. Two years later, he once again used the AGM to argue that businessmen knew better than civil servants how to secure export orders, and that hothouse forcing by officialdom would simply cause overseas sales to wither. With shipping space at a premium, not least because of the high attrition rate in the merchant marine during the war, it remained especially tricky to secure the licences necessary to export goods. The process was so bound up in administrative regulation that one trade journalist commented wryly that as far as the toy industry was concerned the word 'licence' was Greek for unobtainable.[28] As far as government was concerned, however, Walter's strictures fell largely on deaf ears. Following a financial crisis in 1947, and a particularly harsh winter, the monthly export target for the toy industry was raised to £420,000, a figure that was reached only once before it was lowered in 1949 to £350,000. Nevertheless, in 1951 Britain exported toys to the value of £6,850,000, a doubling since 1948. That some of the increase was due to the devaluation of sterling in September 1949 was a consideration which the industry's over-enthusiastic and self-congratulatory champions tended to overlook, but the sheer scale of Lines Brothers' operations, coupled with the quality and reputation of Tri-ang toys, ensured that the company contributed significantly to this total. Indeed, almost as soon as hostilities ceased in 1945, Arthur was dispatched to South America in the hope of opening up new markets, while the establishment of the new Welsh and Northern Irish factories was undertaken in part with an eye to meeting overseas demand. A surviving list, undated but probably from the early 1950s, shows that Lines had agents or representatives in seventy-eight countries, although sales could not have been significant in sparsely populated and poor areas such as Northern Borneo, Eritrea, Salvador, Sierra Leone, and Spanish Honduras. Interestingly, there was no reference to any presence in either France or Germany, while high-protective tariffs still made it difficult to penetrate the lucrative American market, although sales of Tri-ang's top-of-the-range items were sufficient to warrant establishing an American-based selling organisation with its own showroom and warehouse.

It was not only finished goods that contributed to Lines' overseas trade. Bulky items in particular incurred high freight charges and had to contend with the persistence internationally of wide-ranging protective tariffs. It was sometimes cheaper, therefore, to export the materials and parts: indeed it was later claimed that in the postwar years these contributed more to Lines' export sales than finished goods. Once at their destination the parts of course had to be utilised in situ, leading the board, prompted as always by Walter, to consider the benefits of developing additional production facilities overseas, inside national tariff barriers and often with better access to raw materials. There was nothing novel in this but now, as a general policy, it undoubtedly derived added impetus from the complexities involved in exporting and the persistent uncertainties about raw material supplies.[29] Given that Lines' main overseas markets had traditionally been in former imperial territories, where the British roots of many of the inhabitants engendered some sort of sentimental attachment to Tri-ang, it was logical that the initial thrust of the firm's international manufacturing expansion should follow the same pattern.[30] The first venture was in New Zealand, where a ban on toy imports remained in place well into the 1950s. As early as 1946, a local company called Joy Toys was purchased along with a logging mill to provide timber. By 1947, Lines had raised the firm's capitalisation from £12,000 to £250,000, and the original workforce of just half a dozen women had grown to sixty-five, making a thousand items a day on a site in Tamaki.[31] In the same year a Canadian factory was bought, again with a wood mill to take maximum advantage of the copious supplies of local timber. Showrooms were opened in Montreal, Vancouver and Toronto and the whole effort was supported by a substantial team of travelling salesmen. Production began in 1948 under the Thistle label, a sentimental throwback perhaps to the days of G. & J., and reached £2,000,000 by the end of 1949, although substantial start-up costs had to be written off, and the operation struggled for profitability thereafter.

Nevertheless, the Tri-ang Board was optimistic enough to seek additional capital by announcing a new share issue. Half a million 4.5 per cent 20/- (£1.00) preference shares were offered at 22/- (£1.10), together with 150,000 ordinary 5/- (25p) shares at 55/6- (£2.77½p). Intended in part to fund existing and planned overseas developments, they were snapped up by investors convinced by the company's performance and confident of its future prospects. In the last two years of the war, the annual profit had hovered around the £50,000 mark but by 1948 the figure had climbed sharply to £148,000 and Walter boasted that Lines had never been in a stronger position to produce economically and compete in all the markets of the world.[32] True, he was operating in a seller's market but the upward trajectory was still impressive, given the persistence of international trade barriers and, at home, the prevailing levels of taxation and excess profit duty. There was also the consideration that toy prices were still centrally controlled. From July 1947 onwards, the price was 'maintained' or fixed according to a formula based on the cost of production plus six per cent, to which was added an additional margin for the distributor. Despite his vociferous criticism of government interventions in the market, Walter was vigilant in his efforts to ensure that retailers did not seek to sell Tri-ang goods below the maintained price. A 1951 Board of Trade report noted that Lines Brothers was very active in this respect, being 'very dictatorial in their attitude to their retail agents'. It went on to explain that retailers usually put up with this without protest because it was 'generally agreed that other manufacturers cannot compete with Lines Bros on price and quality.'[33]

Part of the capital raised by the new share issue funded the company's next overseas purchase – in Australia. For some years Lines had been trying to buy into Cyclops, a long-established local manufacturer of wheeled toys, several of which seem to have been direct copies of Tri-ang products, but not until 1951 was a fifty per cent interest secured in what then became Cyclops and Lines Brothers (Australia). It was a timely acquisition. Australia was Lines' largest postwar export market but it threatened to disappear when in 1952 the Australian Government, alarmed by the country's rising volume of imports, imposed restrictions leading to a reduction of about eighty per cent in total toy imports. South

Africa, by contrast, had been Lines' largest export market *before* the war, but the challenge there now was the existence of an embargo preventing foreign firms from establishing manufacturing enterprises within the country. Lines circumvented this barrier in 1954 by buying Jabula, an established local manufacturer of metal toys and other goods similar to Lines' own products, albeit of an inferior quality. Having acquired the firm's plant in Johannesburg, Lines secured a second factory in Durban and immediately set about improving the skills of the workforce and the management, as well as enhancing the quality of the products.

But if overseas expansion, whether realised or prospective, helped fuel Walter's optimism in 1949, it in no way reduced his constant chafing against external constraints. He could rarely resist the temptation to take a swipe at government, as in December 1952 when he told shareholders that 'when trade throughout the world returns to freedom from interference by governments the products of your company will be in even greater demand.'[34] But after thus rehearsing his familiar mantra at the AGM, he announced that the company was by now doing so well that it could afford to repeat the general staff bonus paid the previous year. *The Times* was in a similarly optimistic mood, suggesting that the improved quality and availability of toys promised the best Christmas since the war.[35] When the 1953 budget took 6d (2½p) off income tax, reduced the purchase tax on toys (which had been as high as fifty per cent in 1947) and finally abolished excess profit duty, the conditions were created for a second successive bumper Christmas period. Despite occasional fluctuations the domestic market proved particularly vibrant through the rest of the decade, with total consumer expenditure rising by about thirty per cent from 1951 to 1960 and personal disposable income growing at an annual average of just over two per cent between 1948 and 1958. As far as children were concerned, it was estimated that toys accounted for half of the £20 or so per head being spent annually on them by 1956.[36] At the same time, however, the upper parameter of childhood was retreating as adolescence advanced towards it – witness the decisions of the Boy Scouts Association to abandon its members' traditional shorts in favour of long trousers, the BBC's to terminate radio's long-running *Children's Hour*, and the foundation garment industry's to target pre-pubescent girls. It was also the case that the proportion of the population aged under 14 was down to twenty-two per cent compared with thirty-three per cent in 1900. On the other hand, the number of potential buyers of toys was boosted by the fact that virtually all children aged between 12 and 14 were now at school as against only about forty-two per cent half a century before, while the continuing fall in mean family size meant a reduced reliance on passed-down toys.

Tri-ang was ideally suited to take advantage of these conditions and the firm's claim to be the world's largest maker of toys and prams – which was plastered all over its stand at the first postwar BIF in 1947 – was formally endorsed by no less an authority than *The Times* a few years later.[37] Although new plants were being opened or planned both abroad and at home, and the Unique and Unity Cycle Company was rehoused in modern premises in Birmingham, Merton remained at the heart of the Lines empire. Visiting the site in 1950, a trade journalist reported that it covered 750,000 square feet in which 500 power presses and 1,000 hand presses occupied the services of 200 skilled toolmakers.[38] By 1955, over 4,000 of the several thousand employees working in Lines' thirteen plants were at Merton. Tri-ang toys dominated the home market and accounted for between a third and a half of the nation's toy exports, then worth almost £7,000,000. Information prepared for a sales drive in America in 1956 claimed that each year the group was making 10,400,000 miniature mechanical cars, 750,000 bicycles, scooters, and toy automobiles: 1,000,000 wheels and 62,500,000 gear wheels. In the process, it was using 312,000 gallons of paint, 30,000 tons of plastic powder, 25,000 tons of steel, and 3,000,000 square feet of plywood.[39] Most other leading British toy makers were identified with two or three main products – Britains had its lead figures, Meccano its construction sets, Hornby trains and diecast Dinky vehicles, Merrythought its soft toys, Airfix its plastic kits. But while Lines certainly had its own iconic products, it was by this time turning out no fewer than 1,500 different items.

The product ranges had been radically revised and standardised at the end of the war, and the first comprehensive postwar catalogue included a new range of animated wooden toys for younger children and also revamped Minics, some now made of plastic and marketed under the Penguin name. Among the most appealing novelty toys were the Jabberwok clockwork alligator and Wakouwa, a small articulated figure which collapsed when the base on which it stood was depressed. Its success sparked so many imitators that Lines had to threaten legal action against the pirates. The public's wartime familiarity with the ubiquitous US Army jeep inspired a new pedal car, although the subsequent electrification of some of the other more conventional saloon models merely drove up their price. A miniature petrol engine made by IMA for a special FROG model was also expensive, although at 75/- (£3.75) it was probably aimed more at adults anyway. An experiment with radio-controlled boats failed because the instructions proved too complicated for children to follow, but a range of electric-powered plastic models fared much better. They were sold under the Penguin label although the plastic aeroplane kits, which had originally carried that name, vanished altogether after a final advert appeared in *Meccano Magazine* in November 1947.[40]

It is possible that their disappearance reflected the departure from IMA of both Mansour and Wilmot who may have felt some responsibility when evidence emerged of financial dishonesty on the part of some their employees. Arthur's son Richard later suggested that their resignations in 1944 deprived IMA of 'its inspiration for novelty', hence the subsequent phasing out of the Penguin kits, but there was more to it than this.[41] The official embargo on the use of plastic in toys was lifted by August 1945, but the components of plastic itself were still in short supply. Thus the models in IMA's new Penguin Series 9 of construction kits, advertised in December 1945, were composed mainly of wood with metal landing gear and only the propellers and tail wheels made of acetate. Although additional plastic models were available from 1946, the packaging and art work still remained minimal. With exports a priority and demand so high, the hand-packed parts were simply crammed into boxes rather than being held in place by elastic bands as in prewar times. Undue haste often led to some being placed in the wrong box, or even omitted altogether; a deterioration in the quality and standards to which customers had been formerly accustomed and to which the parent company remained publicly committed.

Even without these problems, IMA's use of manually operated Reed-Prentice moulding machines put Penguin at a significant cost disadvantage compared to the growing number of rival American plastic kit producers deploying much faster Lester machines. Although IMA did have a number of such machines, the Lines board was unwilling to support the expensive retooling, which would have been necessary to deploy them on making Penguin aeroplane kits, because it had other more ambitious plans for their use. Whatever the ostensible reason behind the resignations of Mansour and Wilmot, it seems likely that their own aspirations no longer suited Lines. Almost as soon as they left, it was announced that IMA would henceforth function as the Lines Brothers plastics division, a widening of activities perhaps well-symbolised in the appointment of Alan Cathcart, formerly Tri-ang's export manager, as IMA's general manager. As well as making entirely new ranges of plastic toys, IMA's plant was increasingly used to support Minic and Pedigree products. The Pedigree company itself was dissolved, formally ceasing to trade on 31 December 1949. Since 1947, its post-tax profits had averaged out at a modest £6,770, well below the pretax figure of £22,730 achieved in 1950 by another Lines subsidiary, the Unique and Unity Cycle Company.[42] Pedigree's assets and liabilities were transferred on 1 January 1950 to IMA for just over £43,300, a sum that the Lines board proposed to treat as an interest-free loan.

The Tri-ang display at the 1951 BIF included fifty completely new items along with the familiar brands of FROG, Penguin and Minic. The latter retained such cachet that at the end of the decade Minic Ltd. was formed as a separate company and production shifted to Canterbury. Perhaps one of the most appealing Minic innovations was a series of waterline ship models complete with harbour accoutrements. These made for attractive shop displays when set against background scenery provided by Young and Fogg, which was purchased by Lines in 1958 as the UK's largest maker of rubber toys but soon refocused on producing rubber goods for the group's other subsidiaries. Other new lines in the 1950s included miniature versions of household items such as the washing machines (sold complete with a packet of Persil washing powder) and vacuum cleaners then becoming more commonplace in

British homes. An earlier range of push-along animals made of vinyl was neither tactile nor handsome, in complete contrast to the several thousand Pedigree dolls a day being rotationally cast from latex and polyvinyl chloride by 1954. Doll production accounted for two-thirds of IMA's turnover by 1960, and Lines claimed to have the only factory in the world capable of making a complete doll with clothes, wigs, voices and moving eyes. By this time, only about a quarter of IMA's turnover came from Penguin boats and FROG planes, although in the opinion of one Lines' traveller, sales of the latter could have been higher. He took it as axiomatic that the actual kits were superior to those of their main rivals, Keil Kraft, but he suggested that the advertising of the latter was more eye-catching and the information on its packaging more appealing to potential purchasers because it was more direct and more clearly laid out.[43]

A further tenth of IMA turnover was generated from work subcontracted to it by the parent company for Minics, and increasingly for trackside models intended for Tri-ang railways, one of Lines Brothers' most successful postwar initiatives. In the 1950s, model trains were thought to be the world's second most popular hobby after stamp collecting, with the British market dominated since the 1920s by Meccano's Hornby trains. In 1951, Lines purchased Rovex, a Richmond-based plastics company which had a deal to supply Marks & Spencer with injection-moulded plastic toys, including a train set. However, cash flow problems and technical difficulties arising from the company's limited number of injection-moulding machines and tooling expertise, led to the cancellation of the contract. Lines moved in, appreciating from experience that as a modelling medium, plastic lent itself to much finer detailing than the metal still being used by Hornby. The relative cheapness of the actual manufacturing process brought the resulting range of Tri-ang trains within the financial reach of many more potential consumers, and they were marketed so effectively that even the very first brochure proclaimed them to be already the sector leader in terms of value, service and quality. Hornby was left struggling in the wake of what one enthusiast later described as 'the most successful British model railway system in the history of toy making', while smaller competitors such as Trix simply went to the wall.[44] So rapid and comprehensive was the newcomer's success, with additional items being added at such bewildering speed, that within three years a new dedicated factory had to be erected in Margate, selected in preference to a site in Hastings, which would have needed more preparatory work and cost four times as much.[45] Rovex's original Richmond factory was initially given over to the production of musical toys, parts of the Minic range and pilots for some experimental electronic toys, before making way for the manufacture of fibreglass prams. At the end of 1956, having already bought up the remaining share capital of its first Australian subsidiary Cyclops, Lines Brothers purchased Moldex, a Melbourne-based plastics firm then in receivership. From this additional factory, housing what were then the largest injection-moulding machines in its entire organisation, Lines proceeded to turn out Tri-ang versions of Australian trains as well as Pedigree dolls.

At home, Tri-ang's salesmen were instructed to push the new trains in every possible venue, further increasing their competitive advantage over Hornby, which were not only more expensive but also available only in a very restricted and by now rather outdated number of Meccano-approved retail outlets. Lines secured an additional retailing boost in 1957 with the purchase of Simpson, Fawcett & Co, the Plymouth-based makers of Swan prams. The main rationale behind this transaction was to gain control of a major competitor whose wooden-bodied prams complemented Lines' own ranges of steel and, increasingly, fibreglass products. But the deal also included Simpson Fawcett & Co's chain of sixty-eight Youngsters toy and pram shops. Lines moved Simpson Fawcett's manufacturing work to Merthyr and provided the retail chain with a new warehouse and head office on the Merton site adjoining the IMA factory. This excursion into the retail sector complemented not only the group's ownership of Hamleys but also another significant shift in its approach to distribution, the launching of an in-house toy fair in 1955.

Walter had always been an enthusiastic advocate of the BIF as the industry's annual showcase, but the timing of the first postwar fair in May 1947 was too late in the year to enable manufacturers to fulfil orders placed for the following Christmas season. Consequently, Walter and the BTMA council pressed the Board of Trade for a change of date. However, the success of the long-standing, independent Manchester Toy Fair – in fact held in Leeds in 1948 and then from 1950 in Harrogate – led to some rethinking. Walter had never been a fan of this event, regarding it as primarily for the benefit of wholesalers and importers: he effectively scuppered advances from Toy Fair (Manchester) Ltd for collaboration with the BTMA by demanding that, if there were to be any such co-operation, the chairman of the organising committee must be a member of the manufacturers' association. As no doubt he hoped, this was enough to deter any further discussion. In the meantime, the BTMA decided to run its own fair at Brighton as the shop window for British toy manufacturers, backing it with a new journal, *British Toys*. Neither of the first two such fairs was particularly successful and with rumours circulating that the date of the BIF might after all be changed, BTMA members questioned the wisdom of proceeding with a third event in Brighton in 1956. Walter interpreted this as vote of no confidence and promptly resigned his presidency, a decision he refused to reconsider. With Brighton unsuccessful, Harrogate unacceptable, and the timing of the BIF uncertain, Lines Brothers decided to stage its own independent display in London, where it had already opened a much-enlarged showroom some years before. It was a prescient – or lucky – decision because just as the BTMA, having lost its most powerful personality, agreed to merge its own fair with a rescheduled BIF, the government announced that after 1956 it would no longer fund the latter. Attendance at the first Tri-ang fair in 1956, some 2,800, was certainly much lower than the 13,000 who went to that year's BIF, although that, of course, had never been exclusively for the toy trade, but Walter claimed that Lines had taken £1,000,000 worth of orders, far exceeding anything his firm had ever secured at a trade fair. On that basis, he indicated that Lines Brothers would not participate in future BTMA fairs.[46] Attendance and business at Tri-ang's next event the following year were similarly encouraging when many new toys were introduced, most of them also on show at the eight provincial fairs which the company proceeded to organise. The main London exhibition became an annual occasion, even though according to one Board of Trade official both it 'and Mr Walter Lines' rugged individualism generally, tend to be resented in the toy trade.'[47] Resented or not, Tri-ang's initiative was subsequently copied by several other major British manufacturers.

Among the new toys on show at the various Tri-ang fairs held in the second half of the decade, two in particular stood out. Perhaps it was the relative ease with which Meccano's Hornby trains had been sidelined that lured Lines into invading another segment of the market in which Meccano had also long been the leader. Diecast miniature vehicles had long been synonymous with Dinky, first sold under that name in 1934 and widely acknowledged as realistic, high quality and well-finished products. Their supremacy had been pretty much unchallenged until Lesney's Matchbox models appeared on the market in 1953. Although – or perhaps because – these were miniatures they enjoyed great popularity, especially in the tough American market. So, too, did Mettoy's Corgi range, introduced in 1956, and in terms of scale and design more directly competitive with Dinky. Lines was thus relatively late into the field in launching its Spot-On brand in 1959, through a new company based in the Belfast factory. Incorporating moulded interiors and in some models battery-powered headlights, they differed from their competitors in that all were made to a constant scale and used the colour schemes of the real vehicles. These distinctive features, however, tended to push up their price, while the concentration on British vehicles limited their overseas appeal, especially in the United States.

Much more successful was the outcome of another acquisition. Formed by Bertram Francis in 1947, Minimodels Ltd. manufactured tinplate toys, including accurate scale models of racing and sports cars. Most appeared under the brand name Scalex, and many had a fifth wheel in the base which, when the vehicle was pulled backwards on a hard surface, wound up a clockwork motor. Although quality control tended to be poor and wastage rates very high, at its peak Minimodels was turning out 7,000 items a week, and in 1957 Francis moved his operation to Havant. At that year's Harrogate Toy Fair, he exhibited a new product, Scalextric. Inspired by seeing continental battery-powered cars running round a track but without any user control, he had adapted one of his own models for a small electric motor, and then created a track containing metal slots to pick up electric current directed to it through a controller which he also designed. His new tinplate cars, however, were quite crude and did not hold the track very well, their plastic drivers were little more than ill-defined blobs, and the controllers allowed no variation of speed. Nevertheless, with British motor racing enjoying something of a golden era, here was a product with obvious potential and one which expertise in miniature electrics and plastic could enhance. Purchasing Minimodels in 1958, Lines rejigged the drivers to provide them with facial features and hands, increased the number and types of cars, made them of plastic, and improved their design to give them greater track adhesion. Lines even deployed the same system with some success for a new roadway set to increase the play value of the Minic range of vehicles. The most important innovation of all, however, was the provision of a variable speed controller which, in theory at least, greatly added to the realism of the cars' performance. The product's appeal was further increased by the addition of a host of trackside features. So rapidly and comprehensively was the whole system updated and improved that the first catalogue, published in 1960 as a single folded page, had grown by the following year to twenty-four pages.

By the time this publication appeared, Walter had announced his retirement as joint managing director of Lines Brothers. Although he was to remain as chairman of the board, his eldest son, Walter Moray, was left as the sole chief executive. Known in the family as Sandy, he inherited an organisation with 16,000 employees working in thirty-nine factories. The Merthyr plant alone, second largest in the group, was turning out 1,000 prams a week, which together with its metal toys made up an annual production worth £2,000,000, ten per cent of it exported.[48] All told, about sixteen per cent of the Lines group's output was being sold overseas, with wood and metal items accounting for about forty per cent of this, dolls and soft toys for just under twenty per cent, and plastic goods for between eleven and twelve per cent.[49] Although sixteen per cent was well below the industry average of about twenty-five per cent, the sheer volume of Lines' output meant that its absolute contribution to the industry's total exports – worth about £9,250,000 in 1960 – was significant. But perhaps by the same token, quantity seems sometimes to have been achieved at the expense of quality. In June 1958, for instance, the Export Services Branch of the Board of Trade forwarded to Merton details of numerous complaints made about exported Kastor-Kar and Pedipac pushchairs, which were too often arriving at their destinations with jammed wheels, badly fitting tyres and even signs of rust. The UK consul general in Munich urged the board to remind Lines formally that unless there was a qualitative improvement it would be difficult to maintain sales in the highly competitive German market.[50] Shortly afterwards, the Board of Trade was contacted by the UK's trade commissioner in Hong Kong about defective Lines' bicycles. There had been a number of such complaints from local dealers, he explained – 'an interesting commentary on the quality of Tri-ang toys'.[51]

A number of the factories for which Moray Lines now assumed overall responsibility were of course located overseas, including by this time some based in Europe. The decision to establish manufacturing plants in former empire countries after 1945 had initially been driven by the need to overcome shortages of raw materials and high freight costs, and to bypass international tariffs. In his statement to shareholders at the 1956 AGM, Walter suggested that this policy had been amply vindicated by their overseas businesses' growing contribution to the consolidated balance sheet: Joy Toys, for example had expanded its workforce to 216, and the number of its toy lines to more than 300. Two years later he was even more positive, pointing out that after several years of struggle, better sales figures had been returned in Canada, Australian sales improved and a night shift had been introduced in New Zealand to cope with growing demand. The workforce in the South African subsidiary had been doubled in size and Arthur was currently in Johannesburg, with a view to initiating production of items for which export licences could not be secured.

But this same statement also pointed to something of a strategic shift when Walter intimated that affiliations were also being sought with foreign manufacturers based closer to home. Europe certainly offered a larger and potentially wealthier market than the less densely populated imperial territories, but the main incentive to invest directly on the continent was provided by the negotiations which culminated in the 1957 Treaty of Rome establishing the Common Market. The British Government's response to the prospect of common tariffs against its exports was to enter a looser European Free Trade Association (EFTA), something which Walter favoured so long as it did not entail any restrictions on trade, as he told civil servants visiting Merton. It was significant, however, that at this same meeting he also asked for official assistance with his own plans to set up a manufacturing operation in France, and thus inside Common Market tariff barriers.[52] This particular plan eventually came to fruition in 1959 when Lines bought the well-known French firm of Établissements Guy, based at Vivors near Lyon. Another French firm making model railways was also purchased and provided with a new factory at Calais employing 325 locals, while later, in 1962, an old Paris firm of Aube Plastiques was acquired and modernised with the latest plastic-moulding equipment to supply the other two French firms with parts. In Germany, a seventy-five per cent interest was acquired in a long-established Bavarian firm of Schowanek GmbH. From Lines' point of view, this deal had the added benefit that Schowanek's specialised and intricate wooden toys had a strong appeal in America, which, despite its tariff walls, was Lines' highest export earner by 1960. A very attractive formal rights offer to shareholders of one for four of the 5/- (25p) shares at 27/6d (£1.37½) each in 1961 was made in part to raise capital to fund further possible investments inside the Common Market, including the co-ordination of all Lines' continental sales, whether exports or manufactured locally, through a network of distribution companies covering France, Germany, Belgium, Holland, Switzerland and Italy. All of this in Walter's opinion represented 'a first-rate investment for the future'.[53]

A different approach was required on the other side of the Atlantic, where historically Lines had mainly exported goods whose distribution and sales were handled by agents. From the second half of the 1950s, this was supplemented by a growing number of licensing arrangements with American manufacturers. Thus one such agreement permitted IMA to make the Ideal Toy Company of America's plastic toys in the UK, while in return the Americans were granted the rights to make Pedigree's twenty-inch walking doll. Lines also secured access to another range of quality American plastic toys when in 1962 it bought A. A. Hales, a British firm which imported them for the wholesaler, Raphael Lipkin.[54] Yet another contract allowed Rovex to manufacture the educational toys made by the famous American company, Lionel, with Lines selling them on a royalty basis in all English-speaking countries outside the USA. In return Lionel selected a number of Tri-ang's best products to sell in America, also on a royalty basis but with a view to progressively taking on their actual manufacture as well. Among the first fruits of this particular deal was a science set on display at the 1962 Nuremburg Fair where the Tri-ang exhibit was so well laid out and extensive that it caught the eye of a local German journalist who commented enthusiastically on its 'careful design and also the considerable selection of excellent toys'.[55]

This endorsement must have pleased Walter, for design had always been his passion, and excellence his aspiration: even now as he contemplated his final departure from Lines Brothers – he had announced at the end of 1961 that he intended to step down as chairman as well – he was planning to occupy his retirement by making small wooden toys. Yet his last months in the chair were not altogether as tranquil as he may have wished. Prompted perhaps by the apparent proliferation of licensing arrangements, together with the recent ventures into diecast and the acquisition of Minimodels, *The Observer* newspaper not only suggested that Lines was becoming more of an imitator than an initiator, but even hinted that the whole enterprise was shaky.[56] Age had done nothing to stunt Walter's prickliness and in some fury he wrote to the BTMA demanding that it take action on his firm's behalf to refute this suggestion.[57] There was also a distinctly edgy tone in his final report to the AGM in July 1962, covering the financial year ending December 1961: at least, he felt it necessary to stress that the trading profit was the highest in the company's history 'in case there are any doubts in the minds of our shareholders'.[58] Yet behind *The Observer's* comments lay the inescapable fact, confirmed by Table 7, that for all the business's scale and growth during the 1950s, its profitability had not grown significantly in real terms or proportionately to investment.

Table 7. Lines Brothers Ltd. Financial Performance 1952–1961[59]

Year	Net Profit (£)	Assets (£m)	Stocks in Hand (£m)	Liabilities (£m)	Overdraft (£m)
1952	271,342				
1953	248,211				
1954	256,390		0.86		0.252
1955	263,051		1.2		0.708
1956	262,268	3.7	1.3	2.3	0.850
1957	261,440	3.2	1.2	2.2	1.15
1958	290,396	3.0	0.93	1.7	0.465
1959	387,723	3.0	0.79	2.2	1.03
1960	684,000	4.0	0.88	1.6	
1961	456,142	5.0	0.87	1.9	

Source: Lines Brothers, *Annual Reports*

Between the start of 1961 and the end of 1963, earnings per share fell by about two-thirds. Furthermore, while the seasonal nature of the trade meant that periodic overdrafts were common throughout the toy industry, Lines' indebtedness – £3,986,000 at 1 September 1961 – was still striking. Walter's confident prediction that it would be covered by the new rights issue was not realised, and the parent company's bank debts remained over £1,000,000 in 1962. There also appeared to be at least an element of truth in the paper's comment about the company's imitative tendencies. Certainly, an approach Walter made personally to the Board of Trade in 1961 inquiring about the possibility of getting orders for scale models of aircraft and tanks might be interpreted in this way since Schowanek had secured just such a contract with the German Government worth DM 500,000. At the very least, it is somewhat puzzling that the chairman of such a large enterprise should have been personally touting for business in this way.

Despite the oddly mixed tones of unease and confidence, most of Walter's remarks at the 1962 AGM were devoted to reviewing the company's history since 1919, an understandable conceit given that this was his final report from the chair. He had every reason to be proud of what he and his siblings had accomplished in bringing pleasure to generations of children and in creating an organisation with a justifiable claim to be the world's first multinational toy manufacturer. He was 80 years old and the last of the brothers to leave. George, who had only been involved since the early 1930s and never as a member of the main board, had resigned as a director of Pedigree in February 1960, when he was in his early seventies. Will, older than Walter and certainly less well-known to the general public, had withdrawn from active participation in the business just after the war, although he had retained his memberships of the main board and also of several subsidiaries. Apart from an appointment by the minister of transport in 1952 to the Central Transport Consultative Committee for Great Britain, Arthur had an equally low public profile. In their own ways, all of the original triumvirate had contributed to the success of the company, Will in getting it started and then helping to steer it through its first two decades, Arthur in managing the main plant and overseeing the administration for forty years or so before he retired in 1961. Nevertheless, it was widely acknowledged that Walter was the main inspirational dynamic. After visiting Tri-ang House in 1960, one senior civil servant summed up his host as tough, hardworking, energetic, and shrewd, remarking that, 'His tenacity is behind the company's astonishing growth. At 78 he still appears in complete control.'[60] A colleague agreed, noting that he was 'an excellent businessman' before adding astutely that 'he has a high opinion of his own importance.'[61] He supported this assertion by citing Walter's past rejection of a CBE because he wanted a knighthood, but other evidence was not lacking. Well after he resigned from the BTMA, for example, Walter seems to have continued to regard that organisation as a sort of personal fiefdom, as his letter demanding its intervention over *The Observer's* derogatory comments in 1962 suggests. Much earlier, in 1957, he had written in similarly imperious vein to demand that it cancel the membership of a firm which had had the effrontery to distribute its own advertising material at the Tri-ang fair.[62] Nor was he in the least embarrassed by a piece of doggerel which appeared in the *London Evening News*. Indeed, he was so taken with it that he had it reprinted in Tri-ang's in-house magazine *Leading Lines* and even forwarded a copy to the permanent secretary at the Board of Trade, Sir

Richard Powell. 'All around the world like vines, Spread the tentacles of Lines. He'll soon be reaching for the moon, the City's No 1 toy tycoon.'[63] Great poetry it was not, but it was a fair enough assessment of Walter's personality and achievements, for as he himself once said with his usual lack of modesty, he could put the rest of the industry into one of his own baskets.[64]

Chapter Five

The Wheels Come Off, 1961–1971

In a very real sense Walter Lines' retirement in July 1962 marked the end of an era, for it was followed in quick order by the deaths of Arthur in December and Will a few months later. Yet Walter's presence still loomed large over the company, and not simply because he remained on the board. His personality was so forceful that it was always likely to transcend the passing of the firm's formal leadership into the hands of next generation of the family, all of whom had, in any case, been thoroughly immersed in its culture and activities since childhood, when they had sometimes been used as guinea pigs to try out new toys. As adults, most of them went into the business. Walter's daughter Peggy, a University of London graduate, became involved when Walter installed her as chair of the Hamleys Board in 1962, by which time she was in her late thirties. Her two brothers, on the other hand, had both joined Lines Brothers at much younger ages and had worked their way steadily upwards. Walter Moray, the elder who replaced his father as chairman, had previously run the Merthyr operation, and had also had a spell in charge of the Canadian business before his appointment as joint managing director in 1961 when he was 39. Younger brother Graeme joined the company after his discharge from the Army in 1946, starting first at Merton before moving to establish a new boat department in the Merthyr factory. He then took over from the plant manager who was peremptorily – and revealingly – dismissed by Walter for being too independently minded. Graeme moved to London where he specialised in sales and marketing, ultimately replacing George Inglis as sales director. A spell in Germany preceded his relocation to Paris in 1961 as joint managing director with responsibility for company affairs in Europe, charged in particular with completing the link up of the various continental sales and distribution companies. Arthur's sons, too, were involved in the business. John Lines succeeded Graeme at Merthyr while Richard's career started in 1948 when, aged 19, he was dispatched to accompany the chief salesman on a trip to revive prewar trading contracts in the Mediterranean and Middle East. The following year he spent two months in the USA with an Anglo-American productivity council team, investigating modern packaging methods. On his return, he was put in charge of Tri-ang Railways and then appointed managing director of Rovex in 1957 when he was 28 years old. By 1958, all four men were members of the main board with each drawing £4,500 a year in salary, three-quarters of what Walter and Arthur were receiving. Peter Lines, Arthur's younger son, was also in the business, ultimately becoming company secretary in the Canadian operation and then of Pedigree in 1967.

The rather tetchy tone of Walter's final report from the chair for the financial year ending December 1961 was undoubtedly prompted by his awareness that, below the surface, some disturbing currents were stirring, as *The Observer* had hinted. Their ramifications emerged more clearly when Moray presented his first report as chairman in the following year. Total group sales for 1962 were slightly up, thanks to an increase in direct exports and better performances by some of the company's overseas operations. However, overseas margins were always lower than those on home sales and the aggregate sales increase was not sufficient to offset rising labour and raw material expenditures in the UK, high development costs in Europe – particularly in Lyons which lost some £360,000 – and bad results both in the United States, where the outsourcing of selling incurred additional costs of £30,000, and in Canada where changes in import duties and exchange rates contributed to a loss of £140,000. The net outcome was that group profit plunged from £456,000 to £283,000 (see Table 8). One consequence was that the bank overdraft at the end of 1962 had reached over £1,000,000, another that the volume of stock in hand was unusually high. Profits would have fallen even further had the board not carried forward over a quarter of the £380,000 worth of tools written off for the year in question. Moray was nevertheless blandly reassuring, asserting that while the old guard may have departed, the next generation was 'determined that by no step of ours shall the Company fail to progress with equal vigour in the future.' He did, however, concede that in its enthusiasm to capitalise on what he referred to as 'certain opportunities', a young and ambitious board had perhaps 'kicked the ball a little too far ahead' before stressing that it was 'now being firmly gathered in, and strong forward pressure resumed'. The gathering in entailed closure of the Lyons plant, selling the Montreal factory and relocating Canadian production to smaller and cheaper premises, and the resumption of direct control of sales in America. The forward pressure involved a rigorous economy drive to reduce overheads and restrict capital expenditure, the writing off or sale of stocks and tools, the elimination of unprofitable lines, and the simplification of administration throughout the business. Neither directors nor ordinary shareholders were spared, the former accepting salary reductions until profit levels were restored, the latter seeing their annual dividend reduced by a quarter in order to maintain the company's cash reserve. Moray predicted that, cumulatively, these measures would produce improvement in 1963 and a return to what he called 'full flood' the year after.[1]

The anticipated profit improvement for 1963 did materialise, but it was only marginal and would have been smaller still but for another accounting change in the method of charging tool depreciation. More disconcerting perhaps was the disclosure that the most significant contributions to the profit line had come from the subsidiary businesses most recently added to the Lines empire, and that servicing the bank overdraft, which at one point stood at £2,600,000, cost some £275,000. By the following year, however, the figures did seem to be bearing out Moray's confident prediction. Despite reduced earnings in the Antipodes and Germany, and losses in other parts of Europe and America, he was able to report that all the group's constituent companies had improved their performance and contributed to a healthy net profit of over £500,000. Certain that this recovery would be maintained, the board recommended an increased dividend.

Yet Moray added one important caveat to his report when he referred to the additional burden likely to arise from the recent acquisition of Meccano Ltd. Predictably, the new regime at Lines Brothers had

Table 8. Lines Brothers Ltd. Results for Year ending 31 December 1961–1970

Year	Net profit (loss) (£)	Net pre-tax trading profit (£)	Overdraft (Lines Brothers & Subsidiaries) (£)
1961	456,142	1,675,156	212,646
1962	283,005	1,092,958	1,992,909
1963	317,814	1,144,908	4,238,031
1964	536,300	1,061,222	4,896,959
1965	497,979	1,347,344	5,312,186
1966		1,604,455	6,967,901
1967		1,271,829,	5,340,100
1968	748,000 (Lines and Subsidiaries)	867,000	7,221,000
1969	(121,000)*		7,586,000
1970 (to 30 June)	(779,000)		

Source: Lines Brothers, *Annual Reports*
* This became a loss of £300,000 after the payment of preferential dividends.

seen no reason to depart from the company's established practices of manufacturing under licence or buying up other businesses with attractive products. One deal in 1963, for instance, made Lines the sole licensed agent outside the US for goods made by the Deluxe Reading Corporation of America and, ultimately, was to allow the takeover of the Americans' existing assembly and manufacturing facilities in Britain and Holland. Similar arrangements were subsequently made with Joy Toys, Playskool and Craftmaster, while yet another licensing contract gave Lines the manufacturing rights to a range of swimming pools designed for garden use. Available in three sizes, with the most expensive costing over £300, Solido Pools were said by a company spokesman to be well within reach of the average wage earner in Britain.[2] Domestic swimming pools were certainly a logical enough product for a business with a long history of making garden play equipment, but the spokesman hardly seemed to have his finger on the pulse of contemporary reality, given that in 1966 the average wage in the UK was just under £800 a year.

As for direct acquisitions, the company added to its overseas holdings in the course of the decade by buying significant interests in Steelcraft Ltd., an Australian pram maker, and in Regal Trading, South Africa's largest toy wholesaler. Within Britain itself, legal innovations and changes in the international trading environment prompted a surge in the number of company takeovers, which averaged some 890 a year between 1963 and 1968.[3] Lines' contributions to this figure included not only Meccano, but also Shuresta, a Coventry-based firm making bike stands and the Cumfifold range of prams and pushchairs, Walker Industries in Ireland, A. A. Hales, a forty-nine per cent stake in Subbuteo Ltd., and a fifty per cent interest in G. & R. Wrenn. Wrenn made the 152 Series Racing Car system, a leading rival to Scalextric and which was quickly withdrawn from sale after Lines became involved. However, this particular transaction was not nearly as nakedly predatory as this might suggest, for it was actually George Wrenn who took the initiative in approaching Lines. His firm's main product was model trains and, shortly after Lines bought Meccano, he inquired if he could buy the tooling for the Hornby trains which Lines had decided to abandon and, working within the Lines group, assemble them for sale under his name. This clearly made financial sense since it allowed Lines to cash in on a significant quantity of redundant equipment that would otherwise have been scrapped.[4]

Yet the benefits of buying Meccano in the first place were by no means so clear-cut to business commentators who were left scratching their heads when the purchase was announced in 1964. *The Economist* described it as 'one of the strangest ever made' and queried whether it represented good value, given the outlays Lines was already incurring in Europe, and the fact that at home costs were outstripping prices.[5] The *Daily Express* agreed, labelling it as 'one of the oddest ever takeover deals' and it certainly contained elements of irony: it was, after all, a mirror image of the transaction said to have been contemplated by Walter Lines in the 1930s, and it was also the phenomenal success of Tri-ang trains which had to a large degree contributed to Meccano's difficulties in the first place.[6] However, the press reaction was prompted more by surprise that the Meccano board was prepared to accept an offer valuing its shares at less than half their current market value. But the company had been struggling with declining profits for several years and was predicting a loss of £250,000 for the year ending in January 1964. Those in the know were also aware that two years' supply of unsold Hornby trains were already stockpiled, that £600,000 would have to be written off in tools and stocks, and that no dividend would be payable. In that context the price of Meccano shares appeared unrealistic to chairman Roland Hornby and he recommended acceptance of the Lines' offer as 'fair and reasonable'.[7] Even on these terms, the deal still cost £781,000, but Moray had no doubts that it was a bargain, dismissing as nonsense one journalist's suggestion that he had paid too much and claiming that Meccano was 'a fine acquisition'.[8]

In justification, he pointed out that a main attraction of the deal was the opportunity to merge Meccano's well-established operation in France with Lines' own Calais factory to form the largest toy producer in that country. There were other potential benefits too. Cost reductions could be achieved by eliminating overlapping activities. Thus, Meccano's London showroom was moved to Tri-ang House, and its London shop to Hamleys, while in 1967 it was announced that the long-running *Meccano Magazine* was being closed down – Lines had been publishing its own *Tri-ang Magazine* since 1964. There was equal scope for rationalisation with respect to products. Lines' Pennybrix building set was very similar to Meccano's Cliki, while another Meccano construction toy, Bayko, was quietly killed off altogether. Meccano also sold Circuit 24, a slot car racing system originating in France where it was extremely popular, and although it was technically inferior to Scalextric the opportunities for production economies between the two were considerable. As for train sets, Tri-ang already led the market, but by terminating manufacture in Liverpool and rebranding its own models as 'Tri-ang Hornby', Lines was able to capitalise on the reputation of the Hornby name, even though the product bore little relationship to the original.

The process worked in reverse, however, when it came to diecast vehicles. Lines' own Spot-On range had proved expensive, but now production could be quietly subsumed under the older and better-established Dinky brand. Particularly in America, where there was an apparently insatiable demand for British diecast, Dinky sales had suffered badly from what Graeme Lines described to the British commercial attaché in New York as 'hair raising' marketing deficiencies. But by the early summer of 1964 a new organisation had been established under Lines' aegis to sell Dinky in the US, along with car track and a new metal construction kit currently being designed. Graeme, who had been installed as Meccano's managing director after the takeover, also told the attaché that Hornby trains and traditional Meccano construction sets could not compete against local products in America, but he took a much rosier view of the prospects for Meccano sets in the British market.[9] The *Daily Express* might have been sceptical on the grounds that 'hardly anyone bothers to build cranes anymore', but Graeme maintained that the Meccano concept still remained a 'brilliant product'.[10] His confidence was apparently vindicated, for within two years the sets broke all their previous sales records. Graeme later down played his own role in this transformation, rather modestly describing it as being nothing more than sprucing up and adding a few items.[11] The sprucing up included modernising the tooling and improving the finish, while the additions included plastic Meccano and new packaging in the form of shrink wrapping and polystyrene trays.

As well as rationalising and enhancing existing products, Meccano's new managing director was also convinced that the firm's fortunes could be restored, and its potential contribution to the Lines' group profit could be boosted by making production itself more efficient. A surviving memorandum in the Meccano archive projected a gross profit of £788,000 for the year 1964–5, reduced to £82,000 net after overhead costs had been deducted. But £127,000 of these overheads were variable and thus capable of reduction.[12] Meccano's plant was generally old and Graeme aspired to introduce flow line production, suggesting that otherwise the entire Meccano operation might have to be shifted to Merthyr or elsewhere.[13] Although difficulties in securing an appropriate site ultimately forced him to settle for less ambitious change, he was able to reduce the workforce by 1,000 and, in the short term at least, raise productivity. Within four years of the takeover, Lines had converted Meccano's 1963 trading deficit into a profit of £400,000 – although the massive burden of previously accumulated losses remained on the balance sheet, while the persistence of excessively high overheads absorbed most of the potential profit.[14]

The energy with which Graeme Lines initially galvanised the Meccano business was perhaps all the more striking because, as managing director, he went in person to Liverpool for only a couple of days a week, otherwise exercising oversight by letter or telephone. While this seemed to work at the time, it was a practice which served to highlight one of the perils inherent in Lines' continued policy of acquisition and expansion – that of control and co-ordination. Tri-ang's founders had always managed their business in a very hands-on, direct manner. In the early days at Ormside Street and Merton, the brothers had been in the habit of taking frequent and unannounced walks around the shop floors where they were always referred to as 'Mr Will', 'Mr Walter' and so on. This form of address persisted long after the war and was extended to the next generation of the family. But such close personal supervision was unsustainable in the long run because of the way in which the company expanded, both structurally and geographically. Generally, when Lines Brothers opened a new factory it had been Walter's habit – it would be stretching things to call it a strategy – to have it run by senior employees or members of the family. When other businesses were taken over, the practice was to install a family member as managing director and/or pack the board. A 1948 list, for instance, records that Walter, Will, Arthur and Moray were all directors not only of Lines Brothers but also of IMA, Hamleys, the Unique and Unity Cycle Company, Lines Brothers (Wales), Lines Brothers (Ireland) and Pedigree Soft Toys. So, too, was G. F. R. Baguley, who had joined the main board when Lines became a public company in 1933. Walter, Arthur and Moray were also directors of Pearce's, the timber business bought just after the war, as well as the company's offshoots in New Zealand and Canada. Even George Lines, never a member of the main board, was a director at Pedigree and the Unique and Unity Cycle Company. Long-serving employees such as George Inglis, who began his career as one of Tri-ang's first travelling salesmen, eventually became a director of IMA and then joined the main Lines board. George Jones, another of the original trio of salesmen, became managing director of Unique and Unity, while from 1941 onwards, the managing director of Hamleys was an individual who had first joined Lines Brothers in 1927. Alan Cathcart's trajectory was similar. He had started at Lines as a dispatch clerk in 1923, but became a director of IMA in 1947 and of Lines Brothers (New Zealand) in 1954.[15] This helps explain Richard Lines' recollection that when he first started work, daily attendance in Merton's senior dining room was normally about twenty, but that this progressively dwindled as experienced staff and family members alike were dispersed to run new factories or serve on the boards of newly acquired businesses. Overseas commitments, he added, were particularly onerous because most involved time-consuming sea voyages.[16] Yet as Lines Brothers' managing director and chairman Walter had apparently been slow (or perhaps, given his autocratic tendencies, reluctant) to grasp that the growing scale of the business and its multi-site operations made such personal control and supervision increasingly unrealistic, especially as new businesses with different cultures and practices were absorbed. After a lengthy meeting with him in 1960, one civil servant commented that he had had 'no opportunity of judging how far the process of delegation in the Company had gone. It did not appear to have even begun as far as the General Sales Manager was concerned and this could well be a source of weakness.'[17]

Moray, however, did seem inclined to grasp this particular nettle, and in 1964 the first tentative steps were taken to establish a more appropriate management structure when Lines Brothers International was created to co-ordinate the work of the various overseas enterprises. Two years later, the board decided that changes were also required at home. The geographically based entities of Lines Brothers (Ireland) Ltd., Lines Brothers (Richmond) Ltd., and Lines Brothers (South Wales) Ltd., were disbanded in favour of a new divisional structure within which the various subsidiaries were grouped together. Wrenn, Pedigree, Spot-On, Minimodels, and Minic Ltd. were brought together as Rovex Industries, while the various makers of large-wheeled toys were formed into a second division of Tri-ang Toys Ltd. There was little to suggest, however, that in practice this amounted to anything more than rationalisation based mainly on product differentiation, or a mere shuffling of the cards, for the key players remained unchanged. More importantly, perhaps, the basic holding company model of organisation remained intact.

Nevertheless, by the middle of the decade it did appear to outsiders that Lines had recovered from the blip of 1962, so much so that in December 1965 the company's shares were included in a portfolio offered by the Star Unit Fund with an estimated yield of four and three-quarters per cent.[18] Moray's report for that year was correspondingly positive. The loss of the Rhodesian market following that country's declaration of independence in November, and continued difficulties in Canada and France had, he said, been offset by an increase in domestic sales of twenty-five per cent and a rise in pre-tax profit. Although this was not fully reflected in the net profit figure, he concluded that the general position warranted an increase in the annual dividend. Shortly afterwards, however, the government imposed a statutory freeze on wages and prices. This contributed to a rather flat Christmas season and the lower demand for higher priced toys in particular saw Lines' sales and profits in 1966 rise only marginally against the previous year, although the position was somewhat obscured – perhaps deliberately so – by a change in the way the company figures were presented. With substantial stocks of unsold goods in storage, the board agreed to implement a conservative production schedule at the start of 1967. Lines Brothers' reported overdraft in the 1966 accounts was £2,724,691, while the consolidated figure for the group as a whole was £6,967,901, clearly, as Moray said, 'a very heavy charge for the company to carry.'[19] Yet his mood at the 1967 AGM remained bullish and he concluded his remarks on an optimistic note, forecasting a strong upward movement in future profits and offering the reassurance that the board was acting to offset the overdraft: £4,200,000 of additional capital was to be raised by offering a further rights issue to current shareholders and by issuing unsecured loan stock.

The Wheels Come Off, 1961–1971   119

The new rights issue was eagerly taken up and the ordinary shares were sitting at a healthy 32/6d (£1.62½) when, in November 1967, *The Times* published an analysis of the contemporary stock market. Despite the fact that the dividend had been held at the previous year's level, Lines Brothers' shares were recommended as one of the best buys for potential investors, alongside such heavyweights of the British economy as Glaxo, EMI, BP, the Beecham group, and the Pergamon Press.[20] Even at seven and a half per cent, however, the unsecured loan stock was not received so enthusiastically, and only £389,000 of it was taken up, leaving the underwriters with the balance of the £2,000,000. The caution this suggested was probably merited in the circumstances, since for all Moray's confident assertions the first half figures for 1967 showed a loss of £77,000 as against a £202,000 profit in the comparable period for 1966. This disclosure saw the share price drop to 27/3d (just over £1.36) by the end of December. When it emerged that the trading profit for the year was down by about a fifth, the response was yet another reshuffle although the organisational pack was first cut. Shareholders at the AGM in 1968 learned that distribution depots in Nottingham, Market Harborough and Lancashire were scheduled for imminent closure, while a factory at Hayes had already been shut and its production moved to Minimodels at Havant. Work currently undertaken at Canterbury was to be shared between Belfast and Margate to give each more volume, with doll manufacture moving from Merton to Canterbury. Part of the space released at Merton was to be used for storage in order to reduce the rental cost of outside warehousing, part allocated to Ralph Lipkin, the toy-importing business acquired a year or two before. The rest was to be used for the manufacture of new, non-toy products to be unveiled later. These initiatives, Moray suggested, would make for economies by securing greater output from a reduced manufacturing area, although as he went on to point out, they would also incur considerable outlays on redundancy and removals. He further warned that a forthcoming review and cull of product ranges would incur additional losses from the resulting disposal of stock, although these were to be covered from reserves. Admitting that the scale of these various measures would place a great strain on management, he could still not resist adding that he fully expected the company's recovery of 1962–66 to be resumed. His optimism, like his father's, was seemingly irrepressible, but he did at least concede that there could be no guarantees because of what he termed 'the current mismanagement of the country's affairs'.[21]

In making this latter comment, Moray was taking a rather clumsy swipe at the economic policies of the Labour Party, which had won a narrow electoral victory in 1964 and then returned with a much stronger mandate in a general election two years later. Although Lines occasionally contributed to the funds of both the Conservative Party and the right-wing Economic League, the sums involved were minute (around £100) and Moray's remark was more tactical than ideological, intended perhaps to divert attention away from his company's faltering performance. Yet he was not entirely unjustified because, like all businesses, Lines Brothers was being affected by policy-driven shifts in the operating environment, although Richard Lines was mistaken in later suggesting that the abolition of retail price maintenance in 1964 was the only such policy change which impacted Lines at all seriously.[22] A Conservative initiative, this had certainly alarmed all toy manufacturers as it was widely expected that major stores and mail order catalogue companies would use it to demand lower prices for their toy purchases. But in practice most manufacturers coped, following Lines Brothers' example (and the response of many producers in other affected industries) by introducing recommended resale prices. Consequently, the new law made little practical difference in the short term to the industry. However, the Labour Government's ongoing efforts to deal with Britain's balance of payments problems had far more serious implications for the toy trade in general, and Lines in particular. Despite its best intentions and its commitment to a more directly interventionist regime, Labour found itself unable to break out of the stop-go cycle which had emerged in the 1950s as governments tried to address Britain's chronic trade deficits by alternately expanding and dampening domestic demand through variations in tax levels and the bank rate or credit restrictions. In a final desperate attempt to end these recurrent swings, the government announced in November 1967 that sterling was to be devalued, the expectation being that this would provide a welcome and permanent boost to exports whilst simultaneously making imports more expensive. The timing of the decision was too late to have much effect on Lines' figures for 1967, although Moray reckoned that in the longer term it would reduce the price of exported toys by about six per cent and lead to a twenty-five per cent increase in Lines' overseas sales.[23] Strangely, his optimism did not deter him from proposing that the BTMA should seek an increase in the working week because 'the state of the national economy called for drastic action.'[24]

That Britain's balance of payments problem became more acute in the 1960s was in large part a consequence of the way in which barriers to international trade had been progressively whittled away ever since the signing of the General Agreement on Tariffs and Trade in 1947. After the war, a few countries, their numbers subsequently extended over the years, had been allowed token toy sales in Britain as early as 1946. The thirty per cent import tariff on toys imposed after 1945 had fallen to twenty-five percent by 1960, and an equally gradual process led in 1960 to the total abolition of the quotas (except in the case of Japan) governing the quantity of toys any individual country could send to Britain. The consequence for domestic manufacturers was steadily increasing competition, although *The Times* was rather over-egging things when it pointed out that not one of the top London store buyers' recommendations for Christmas toys in 1960 – Lego, a battery-operated elephant from Japan and a highway construction set – was British-made.[25] More pertinent to Lines Brothers was the same paper's observation, twelve months later, that while ninety per cent of toys sold in British shops were indigenous products, in the larger, higher-quality shops of the type traditionally associated with Tri-ang, the proportion was only sixty per cent.[26] Even more alarming, as the decade progressed the volume of foreign toys imported to Britain increased spectacularly, totally unaffected by the temporary imposition of a fifteen per cent import surcharge in 1965 and only marginally by the 1967 devaluation (See Table 9).

Japan had become the world's largest toy exporter by the end of the 1960s but was not a particular concern to Britain because its imports were still subject to quotas. It is true that in his usual imperious manner,

Walter Lines had once demanded that imports of miniature electric motors from Japan be banned on the grounds that they were cheaper than the 10,000 or so his Margate factory was producing each week, but later he dismissed the threat from Japanese toys both at home or abroad because their quality was so poor.[27]

The same was broadly true of toys made in Hong Kong, the world's second largest exporter. It accounted for about forty-five per cent of Britain's toy imports but despite an extensive utilisation of modern machinery, Hong Kong produced primarily small-scale cheap plastic items brought in by wholesalers and not much of a threat to Lines.

The more serious challenge came from the other side of the Atlantic. Louis Marx had set up a factory in Wales just after the war, but the progressive liberalisation of world trade was soon attracting other American toy makers. The tentative exploration of the British market in the 1950s by firms such as Revell and Lindberg (both plastic kit makers) and Baby's Pal prompted one trade journalist to ponder whether this was 'a bridgehead heralding the beginning of a more general American attack.' If so, the writer continued, British makers had better take note because the invaders would bring their own marketing and merchandising methods, thereby exposing indigenous firms which,

Table 9. Total Toy Imports to the UK 1960–1968

Year	Imports (£)
1960	5,230,000
1961	5,930,000
1962	7,280,000
1963	8,420,000
1964	10,940,000
1965	11,240,000
1966	13,850,000
1967	13,820,000
1968	18,130,000

Source: Derived from Board of Trade, Statements of the Trade of the United Kingdom

with some exceptions, were 'singularly backward' in promotional work.[28] This might well have been directed at Lines Brothers whose advertising since the war had been quite minimal and conventional because, as Graeme Lines admitted, the company had been largely content to trade on its name and reputation. However, in December 1956 the firm ran a quarter-of-an-hour feature on commercial television which had been launched fifteen months before. Seen by almost five million people, it resulted in a massive rise in the number of printed catalogues requested by retailers from 250,000 to 800,000. The following year, Tri-ang took ten slots on television during the pre-Christmas months, with Graeme stressing, significantly, that they had opted for this particular form of publicity because it was the American way of doing things.[29] In 1961, the US Department of Commerce helped organise the first American toy show in London. A second followed in 1962 and within a year the American share of the toy imports entering Britain was growing three times faster than those from anywhere else. That this bridgehead would be further consolidated seemed inevitable as a spate of domestic mergers and takeovers in the USA saw the creation of some very large-scale toy conglomerates keen to maximise sales by expanding exports. The particular attraction of the British market lay both in its size and the familiarity of its consumers with the artefacts of American culture. It was widely acknowledged that trans-Atlantic toy makers were superior in technology, packaging, and marketing compared with domestic producers, who were generally thought to be tarred with the brush of tradition and impaired by a lack of imagination. American firms also had a huge advantage in terms of lower costs and thus of pricing, conferred in part by newer and more efficient models of business organisation and, in part, by a lower domestic inflation rate which was about two-thirds of the British level through the 1960s. By 1968, American manufacturers accounted for eighteen per cent of Britain's toy imports, and some, such as the Aurora Plastics Corporation, were setting up production plants in Britain.[30] The fact that both Mattel and the Ideal Toy Corporation persevered despite reporting significant initial losses in the UK market was an indicator of just how determined they were to establish a foothold within it.

As Britain's largest toy manufacturer with about a quarter of the domestic market, Lines was clearly vulnerable to this aggressive competition, particularly as the higher rate of domestic inflation was undermining its cost competitiveness with the Americans. It was also hampered to some extent by its own history. Past commercial success had depended on capturing and then, with the protection of tariffs from the 1930s onwards, maintaining a large home market based on toys which appealed to more than one generation and which could be easily modified and developed. Such goods also had a naturally strong affinity and appeal for populations in former imperial territories which identified with the British way of life, and where Lines developed both production and sales operations. Postwar expansion into Europe, however logical as a means of getting inside common tariff barriers, could not be based solely on such products. Furthermore, while novelty and modification had always been of the essence in the toy market, televised advertising and increased international competition from the later 1950s intensified the urgency with which fresh ideas had to be generated and turned into marketable commodities. It was precisely to help develop new concepts that Lines established a research department in 1964, although oddly it was specifically directed to avoid imitating American trends. Perhaps, too, there was in this initiative a somewhat belated recognition, readily acknowledged later by Graeme Lines, that the company had for too long sustained products that were going out of fashion and that while new products had certainly emerged over the years the old had not been sufficiently pruned.[31]

This suggests that a certain degree of complacency had set in, compounded perhaps by the fact that sales figures, always a key yardstick when Walter was in charge, generally remained healthy. Yet in the past, Lines Brothers had tended to be the pacemaker whether in terms of plant modernisation, the use of new materials such as steel and plastic, and in the 1950s fibreglass, or the application of technology to toys, be it pneumatic tyres, electric pedal cars, or flying aeroplanes. By the 1960s, however, something of the momentum seems to have been lost as the company's dealings with Peter Adolph well-illustrated. Adolph had set up Subbuteo Sports Games to manufacture and market a table football game which he had patented in the late 1940s It proved popular and eventually he purchased the Medway Tool Company, a plastics-moulding business which had, for some years, made the small figures used in his game, and changed its name to Subbuteo Ltd. In 1966, Lines took a forty-nine per cent stake in this firm and contracted it to make the plastic drivers and trackside features for Scalextric. But this was the very year in which England hosted and won the football World Cup, an achievement which so boosted the demand for Adolph's table game that in 1969 Waddingtons bought him out. By then Lines was struggling, but the failure to capitalise on the earlier connection with Adolph's plastic company and secure the game itself does seem to have been something of a missed opportunity.[32] The same might be said of a short-lived collaboration with Moulton, a firm which had pioneered a completely new concept in small-wheeled bicycles, and which Lines approached with a view to producing what was in effect a toy version. The outcome, built in Birmingham by the Unique and Unity Cycle Company, was the Tri-ang Junior Bike launched in 1965, and later the Tri-ang Dragster. Moulton's breakthrough designs, effectively the first significant innovation since the 1880s, proved to have a global appeal, but when the company ran into financial difficulties in 1967, Lines missed the chance – or was by then unable – to come to the rescue and it was Raleigh which stepped in to buy Moulton out.

None of this is to suggest that there was no innovation or product development at all at Lines, although the establishment of an entirely new company in 1968 to market the Copy Mate photocopier proved to be a leap too far for a toy maker. More promising was the production from 1966 onwards of model trains in the liveries of the Canadian National and Canadian Pacific Railways, with the parts manufactured in England for assembly by the Canadian company. Yet even this was a belated initiative as by now model railways were losing something of their appeal. In America, particularly, slot car racing clubs became popular, perhaps luring Lines into launching Super 124 Scalextric in 1968. As a larger-scale version of the original it was inevitably far more expensive, with the cheapest set selling for £22/10/0d (£22.50), the equivalent today of over £400. But in the home market slot car racing clubs were far less numerous and the toy never became to children's play or adult leisure in the UK what model trains had been for the previous forty years. The 124 was a commercial flop and did not last long. Neither, despite widespread publicity, did another innovation first available in the 1970 catalogue, 'You-Steer' Scalextric proving far less exciting than the offer of 'power steering' implied. As the sales figures indicated, Meccano sets did benefit from their upgrading and repackaging, which gave them a far more contemporary appearance, although the product's popularity was waning in the face of competition from Lego: even Meccano enthusiasts had to acknowledge that Lego bricks were easier to use because they 'held together and you didn't have to understand how forces work. Meccano needed a bit of intuition.'[33] Lines' answer to Lego was Arkitex, a new architectural toy which appeared in 1961 but with little success. Although it was available in two scales, one compatible with Tri-ang trains, the other with Spot-On vehicles, the smaller sets allowed only the construction of basic box-shaped buildings and more elaborate features were available only in larger sets. Like Meccano, and unlike Lego, it probably appealed far more to boys than girls. Other new products also did less well than anticipated because they were essentially imitative. This was the case with a board game series launched in 1966, but into a market segment long-dominated by firms such as Chad Valley and Waddingtons. Similarly, a range of small-scale vehicles announced in 1967 under the brand name of Mini-dinkies was, as the name strongly suggested, a rather obvious attempt to cash in on the massive success of Lesney's Matchbox models.

Yet imitation was not always or inherently commercially doomed as the Sindy doll, arguably the Lines group's most successful product of all in the 1960s, proved. Under the Pedigree label, Lines had been making and selling teenage dolls successfully throughout the 1950s and its top-of-the-range Miss Debutante, which launched in 1960, had articulated joints, was fully dressed and boasted such exotic names as Theda and Louretta. Nevertheless, Lines turned down the opportunity to acquire a licence from the American company Mattel to market the Barbie doll, believing that an adolescent figure modelled with the equivalent of a thirty-six inch bust would have little appeal to girls in

Britain where the average female bust measured a more modest thirty-four inches. It was a decision illustrative both of complacency and a certain lack of commercial edge, for within a year of its launch in 1959 Barbie sold 300,000 units. It took Lines four years to respond, with Sindy appearing under the Pedigree label in 1963. Even then it was based on another American doll, Tammy, and even deployed the same strap line of 'the doll you love to dress'. Rather coarsely but accurately dubbed by a German politician as 'Barbie without the boobs', Sindy's success served to underline what an opportunity had been previously missed. The doll was the UK's top-selling toy in 1968 and 1970 but Lines was still playing catch-up rather than leading the field. Mattel introduced Barbie's boyfriend Ken in 1961: Sindy's equivalent Paul did not turn up until 1965: Barbie's sister was born in 1964, Sindy's in 1966. Lines Brothers was even further behind when it came to dolls for boys, eventually losing out to Palitoy in a battle for the domestic production rights in Hasbro's highly profitable Action Man.

Although Pedigree won the advertising award for its Sindy campaign when the British Toy Retailers Association announced the results of its newly established Toy Of The Year awards in 1966, no other Lines product figured in the list. It was symptomatic of how the company was now lagging behind the pace-setters that the award for overall toy of the year and also for the best boy's toy went to Corgi's James Bond car, while Palitoy's Tiny Tears doll was adjudged to be the best toy for girls. Spirograph and Lego shared the prize for best educational toy. Moray Lines was disparaging about these sorts of accolades. Asked in 1970 why only four British-made toys were in that year's list of best Christmas sellers, he replied that 'any one can make a Toy of the Year Award toy – give it heavy advertising, do not deliver it, and say it's so popular it's in short supply.'[34] Yet his words hardly sat well with Lines' own increasingly strenuous efforts to preserve its position, for Christmas 1968 saw its costliest ever television campaign and arrangements made to have the catalogue included with copies of the *TV Times*. It was reckoned that this would put the company's products before twelve to fifteen million people. Over the year as a whole, the Lines group spent more than £348,000 on publicity, massively ahead of anyone else: three other leading British manufacturers, Airfix, Mettoy and Lesney, for instance, spent a mere £129,143 between them.[35] It was indicative of developing internal tensions that Richard Lines had strong reservations about these expenditures, because many of the firm's products, such as heavy-wheeled toys, did not readily lend themselves to the medium. Furthermore, because the sheer number of goods made by the Lines group was now so wide, the campaign tended to lack focus, drawing attention to the maker's name rather than to specific products which children might wish to have.[36]

Whatever the merits of Richard's views, there was certainly some nervous selling of shares prior to the 1969 AGM, prompted perhaps by news that Raleigh, part of Tube Investments, was launching its new range of Dreamline prams with the ambition of securing at least a quarter of the market over next three years or so. That was clearly unwelcome news, given that Lines Brothers accounted for about a half of all pram sales in Britain, which were worth some £8,000,000 annually. Nevertheless, and despite an expenditure of over £700,000 on the radical measures announced the previous year, a consolidated net profit for 1968 of £748,000 caused the share price to steady somewhat. Yet even another change in the format of the accounts could not hide some worrying statistics. One was a drop of more than eleven per cent in the consolidated trading profit: another was a group overdraft of well over £7,000,000. Interest rates had risen steadily since the early 1960s and were currently hovering around seven per cent. With lending ceilings in continuous operation and credit restrictions still very tight, the costs of servicing such a level of debt was a major burden and Moray concluded his annual statement on an untypically sombre note, saying that he did not wish to raise false hopes and that he would issue an interim statement covering the first half of the current year. When that statement appeared, the unaudited figures revealed a half year loss to June 1969 of £118,000, attributable, in Moray's opinion, to the domestic credit squeeze which was driving up the cost of group borrowing to alarming levels. Otherwise, however, he once more sought to emphasise the positives, noting that direct exports had risen significantly and that the current deficit was lower than the equivalent period in 1968, with the main sales period still to come. Somewhat perversely this seems to have worked, for the share price rose from 16/3d (about 81p) to just under 18/9d (about 94p), something *The Times* put down to the chairman's optimistic tone.[37]

Yet this still represented a significant decline in the space of a couple of years, and the first half loss had been incurred in spite of the board's determined efforts to control group borrowing. Tighter financial controls had been imposed, requiring all divisions and subsidiaries to produce monthly profit and loss reports, together with weekly lists of orders, production, wages, and raw material consumption. Although this information kept the board better informed about the company's financial affairs, it could not do much to address the underlying liquidity problem. With every link in the toy trade chain suffering from the effects of the latest credit squeeze, Lines, as the manufacturer, was caught between suppliers pressing for prompt payment and customers seeking extended credit facilities and proving reluctant to settle bills in a timely way. By April 1969, for example, Meccano had 600 blacklisted customer accounts while Tri-ang's own list was even longer, with more than 400 names having been added to it over the previous twelve months alone. When Graeme Lines urged Meccano to make every effort to increase sales and reduce its debtor list, there was a hint of desperation in his final injunction that even small payments would be better than nothing.[38] There was certainly a note of urgency in Moray's confidential memo setting out the contributions each business was expected to make towards generating the £1,500,000 required to bring the group within its legal borrowing limit. Buying was to be cut back, stocks reduced, credit maximised, discounts offered to major customers willing to settle early, and capital expenditures held back. In addition, bills were to be drawn on export customers which the group would discount, while main suppliers were also to draw bills on the group which would be payable from 31 October 1969. By such measures Rovex was to find £440,000, Tri-ang £300,000, Minimodels £245,000, Pedigree £110,000, Shuresta £45,000, Youngsters £10,000, and others £120,000. Meccano's share was to be £150,000.[39] It is not clear how these instructions were received within the group generally, but Meccano's company secretary was simply incredulous. Pointing out that his firm was already failing to achieve either its output or its sales targets and that the requirement for a further £150,000 meant that altogether he was expected to find £337,000, James Mullen airily dismissed the memo, telling Graeme Lines that 'we must be practical and face facts rather than theorise and be disappointed.'[40] Graeme's suggestion that Meccano's focus should be on cutting costs by reducing its excessive staff overheads barely dented Mullen's complacency, producing merely the retort that Meccano's costs relative to budgeted sales were 2.04 per cent, lower than Minimodels (2.63 per cent), Rovex (3.13 per cent) and Tri-ang (2.69 per cent). This rather overlooked the firm's failure to get anywhere near its sales target and Graeme was livid, accusing Mullen of a reluctance to even try to introduce the required economies which were both vital and urgent.[41] In November, Graeme was still ordering him to look 'with extreme care' at the cash flow position in Meccano's budget projections for 1970. He described as 'unacceptable' the company's contribution in the current year of only £174,000 against a budgeted profit of £250,000, a figure which in itself he thought 'rather inadequate'. Without special dispensation from the Lines board, he continued, Meccano must contribute at least £284, 000. 'It is of vital importance that the total Group must make a huge effort in 1970 to get the Cash Flow in the right direction.'[42]

Both Graeme and Moray had clearly imbibed their father's principles when it came to dealing with economic adversity, with Graeme once telling the British Sales Promotion Association that the quickest way to depress a market was 'to look glum, talk of nothing but the bad conditions and lack of money or even to acknowledge its possibility. Businesses have not been built in this way – but rather by optimism and cheerfulness.'[43] It was only to be expected, therefore, that publicly Lines was presenting a rather more positive picture than the underlying trends warranted. Graeme told the *Financial Times* that he was expecting 2,000 customers and a fifteen per cent increase in business at the 1970 Tri-ang Toy Fair, which would see the introduction of four new dolls, a Dinky plane with a retractable undercarriage, and You Steer Scalextric.[44] At the same time, the company was making as much capital as it could from the fact that its proposed advertising budget for the year would be the largest ever seen in the toy trade. Graeme also tried to put a positive gloss on a deal made in January with Benson's Hosiery (Holdings) Ltd., suppliers of non-food items to 5,000 supermarkets and service stations. In the past, Lines Brothers had always been reluctant to supply such general retail outlets, committed as Moray once explained to the view that only specialist toy sellers could provide the expert demonstration and instruction required for many toys.[45] But the firm's need for cash was now so pressing that this principle was effectively being jettisoned, although Graeme's opaque explanation tried to obscure the fact. Like all manufacturers, he said, Lines was under continued pressure to supply grocery outlets and the contract with Benson had been signed 'because we wanted a rational system for meeting this demand and supplying it with special merchandise, while doing minimum damage to the traditional toy trade.'[46]

It was of course a moot point as to what the term 'traditional toy trade' meant by this time. Victorian concepts of childhood on which the Lines' business had originally been built had been progressively diluted from the 1950s and consumer expectations had expanded with rising incomes, while the growing importance of televised advertising which was, in any case, more appropriate to some types of toys rather than others also accelerated the need for novelty and innovation. Above all, the market both at home and abroad had become far more competitive with the liberalisation of international trade, fostering the spread of the more aggressive marketing and sales techniques particularly associated with American business. Marvin Gass, a leading independent toy designer, captured the essential difference between the British and American industries at this time by suggesting that whereas British toy fairs were friendly, congenial and open, one needed to attend their American equivalents 'in a tank'.[47] Effectively, Graeme Lines seemed to accept the truth of this, though couching it in rather more elevated terms by commenting that the American industry was essentially promotional whereas British toymakers were concerned with play value and giving joy.[48] Gass's further comments that the British industry was out of date, derivative, and overly dependent on corporate designers unduly fettered by management might have been too strong and too generalised, but he did make them shortly after Mattel enjoyed a phenomenal marketing triumph with its Hot Wheels diecast vehicles. With incorporated independent suspension, Hot Wheels provided smoother and longer running distances than any other model vehicle on the market and their (literally) runaway success pushed down the 1969 profits of British diecast companies, Lesney's by twenty-nine per cent and Mettoy's by £300,000 in nine months. It was another case of a missed opportunity for Lines Brothers since the concept had first been considered – and rejected – by executives at its Meccano subsidiary.

Largely on the back of this success, Mattel announced a major sales initiative in Britain. Plans to introduce dedicated toy centres and innovative schemes to encourage retailers to take their goods were to be spearheaded by an extensive publicity campaign. Virtually all advertising of toys was by definition predatory, since manufacturers could do nothing to affect either the number of children or available disposable income, which were the two key determinants of the market's size. Coming as it did from one of America's fastest growing toy companies (it had gone public as recently as 1960), Mattel's announcement thus represented a direct challenge to Lines which for all its problems was still the dominant player in British market, where it accounted for almost fifty-nine per cent of turnover in 1968. In an interview which appeared in *Toys International* under the heading 'Lines Bros ready for gloves off battle on world front', Moray responded defiantly to Mattel's plans. In future, he said, Lines would licence fewer American products and concentrate on its own products, arguing that all the good ideas in the industry were British (though only one of the three examples he cited was a Lines' product). While he anticipated a ding-dong battle between the major companies, not all of which would survive, he was confident that Lines would not be among the casualties 'because we have the advantage of a wide base on which to build. Sometimes we are criticised for making too many toys, which could be true, but on the other hand it does give us considerable depth and strength.' Graeme was even more strident in claiming that all the best toy concepts were British and suggesting that the Americans merely added gimmicks to diecast cars, which was far too glib a dismissal of the significant design advance represented by Hot Wheels.

Lines Brothers, he added, was harnessing every resource to combat the American threat and would not look across the Atlantic for ideas. Nor would his family business – which had been a global name before Mattel was even heard of – start advertising like the Americans, preferring instead to make good products that people wanted to buy. 'Lines Bros was established as a power when a fight was needed during the slump. We won that battle. We are used to fighting,' he said.[49]

But these echoes of Churchillian rhetoric clearly belied the reality. For one thing, Lines had already committed itself to the costliest advertising campaign ever undertaken by a British toy manufacturer: for another, group sales for the 1969 Christmas period had fallen disastrously short of projections, making the cash flow situation even more critical. Behind the scenes, the attempts to reduce overheads and indebtedness were continuing apace, albeit still without much success as far as Meccano was concerned. A 1968 analysis of wages across the group's numerous factories revealed that at Meccano the expenditure on non-productive labour was 235 per cent of that on productive labour. The ratios at Rovex and Belfast were not nearly so poor but still adverse at 105 and 107 per cent respectively. Interestingly, and with the exception of the French plant, most of the overseas factories operated far more efficiently than the British ones.[50] In another throw of the dice, therefore, the board turned to PE Management Consultants (PEMC). There followed yet another shuffling of the organisational pack into three divisions –Tri-ang Pedigree, Rovex Tri-ang and Tri-ang Meccano – and a much wider deployment of the familiar Tri-ang label, intended perhaps to restore some sense of collective identity to the group as a whole. To finance this reorganisation, a new reserve fund of some £1,250,000 was to be established, with the balance used to cover the costs of reducing the group inventory by some fifteen per cent. Further recommendations to create a corporate planning department and new financial control systems seem to have been well justified given that Gerald Lucas of the Toy Retailers Association later observed that in the experience of his members, the Lines Brothers' accounts office was inefficient and never seemed to know what the sales department was doing. Agreed discounts, he complained, were often not carried through on paper, while invoicing was often inaccurate.⁵¹ It was significant, too, that the consultants wanted both corporate planning and the new financial system to be run by externally recruited managers. Set alongside their recommendation for the appointment of a new managing director, also from outside the group and with a mandate to introduce modern methods of management, this represented a pretty explicit indictment of the executive deficiencies within the Lines Brothers' organisation which were hindering the business from functioning successfully in the contemporary context.

As already noted, senior management positions throughout the entire business had long been dominated by the Lines family, their original associates, or long-serving employees. The same was also true of the board which, by January 1970, still contained five family members, Bert Munro one of the original directors, G. F. R. Baguley who had served since 1933 and H. K. Babcock, who had started as a costing clerk in 1928 and worked his way up via chief buyer and then managing director of Minimodels. All were steeped in the traditions and culture created primarily by Walter and it is well understood that, once in place, company cultures are hard to shift. In this context, it is worth noting Graeme Lines' characterisation of the veteran sales manager George Inglis, whom he replaced in the late 1950s, as sound but fundamentally still stuck in the past.⁵² Not much seems to have changed by 1969 when R. E. Morgan of Tri-ang Pedigree was seconded to the board along with David Nicolson, chairman of BTR Ltd (the British Tyre and Rubber Company) and something of a business guru with strong links to PEMC. When he joined Lines he was also involved in trying to rescue other ailing enterprises such as Leyland Industries and Shipton Automation.

Furthermore, as Graeme Lines later confirmed, the company's difficulties had exposed differences of opinion at board level and he cited his own resignation brought about, he said, because he could not get his ideas accepted.⁵³ He further suggested that tensions and disagreements were harder to resolve because family members were unwilling to be sufficiently critical of each other, effectively paralysing the board when decisive action needed to be taken. Perhaps he was referring to the fact that he himself was not particularly impressed by the consultants brought in by his brother.⁵⁴ Nor was Richard Lines. Whether he spoke up at the time is not clear, but long afterwards he indicated that he had not been in favour of resorting to them in the first place, damning them as 'failed businessmen' who could not possibly 'know' a company in the same way as those who carried everything in their heads though perhaps not on paper.⁵⁵

At all events, on 1 July 1970 Moray Lines informed shareholders that the board was to be restructured. Walter, Graeme, Richard and John were stepping down, along with three other directors. Newcomers included on a smaller and more compact board included Messrs Fallman and Wadsworth, managing directors of Tri-ang Meccano and Rovex/Minimodels Tri-ang respectively. Moray himself was to remain as chairman but not as managing director, and J. O. Darby, an accountant who had joined the board the previous September to help on the financial side, was to become vice chairman. The finance editor at *The Times* wondered blackly why it had taken so long for the axe to fall, suggesting that few shareholders would 'echo the chairman's remark that he is still glad that he has not sold any of his shares.'⁵⁶ Even Graeme, who was on record as saying that personally he would have liked to buy additional shares, had in fact already sold a substantial portion of them, reducing his holding by over two-thirds shortly before the group's 1969 figures were made public. It did not look good, but the company issued a supportive statement clearing him of any suggestion of insider trading and stressing that his resignation from the board had nothing to do with the disposal of his shares. Graeme explained that the sale had been forced upon him when his bank, after a year of haggling, finally refused to release him from an undertaking to sell his disposable assets in order to clear his personal overdraft.⁵⁷

He may have been able to salvage something from his personal stake in the family business but later, at the AGM, Moray acknowledged that the group's latest set of figures represented a heavy blow and he was 'in no mood to pass it over lightly'.⁵⁸ Superficially, total sales of £38,000,000 appeared impressive, but they hid a disastrous £2,000,000 shortfall in estimated Christmas sales which led to significant increases in stock holdings and the overdraft. Interest and depreciation charges were higher than in the previous year, by £317,000 and £129,000 respectively, to which had to be added the £175,000 written off in launching new products subsequently discontinued. The overall result was a two-thirds drop in pre-tax profit and a dividend of 3d (1¼p) compared to 1/4d (just over 6½p) the previous year. Conscious that such a dismal outcome raised serious questions about his own stewardship of the company's affairs, Moray defended his decision to remain as chairman on the grounds that he felt a sense of responsibility both to the banks, which had supported the group, and to employees and customers, and also because he did not wish to let the shareholders down. Realising perhaps that he was on shaky ground in saying that he would not wish to remain as chairman without shareholder support, he sought to bestow an additional aura of credibility on both his own position and the board's restructuring by referring to his father's continuous and firm backing. Walter, he added, might be leaving the board to become life president but 'he has most strongly insisted that the reorganisation should take place regardless of family and other interests.'[59] The revamped board, Moray went on, provided a good mix of their own best young executives and experienced outsiders, while plans were in hand to appoint both a third non-executive director and a new group managing director in line with the consultants' recommendations. Until that appointment was made, he added, a senior manager from the consultants was helping to expedite the necessary changes. Together with the measures already taken he was confident that the favourable reception of some recent new products, and the establishment of new sales outlets, would bring the overdraft down by the end of the year and in the longer run lead to 'complete transformation'. The current year would be difficult, he warned, but the group's inherent strength was enormous, the foundations of a new structure had been laid and the opportunity had been created to 'build fast and solidly for the future'.[60]

The foundations, however, were crumbling almost as he spoke. The Target Equity Fund may have capitalised on Lines' falling share price to triple its holdings over the course of July, but other institutional investors in the business were far less confident. Led by PRJ Investments, a ginger group of shareholders began pressing for Moray's removal from the chair. The very fact that Darby felt it necessary to issue a statement stressing that the board, the consultants and the group's financial advisers were all standing by the chairman, was in itself a measure of how precarious Moray's position had become. The situation worsened when a six-month statement published in October showed a loss to 30 June 1970 of £779,000 compared to £63,000 for the equivalent period in 1969. Moray offered a crumb of comfort by pointing out that the best part of the selling year was still to come, but the cash flow problem remained unresolved and in September the board moved to increase the group's borrowing powers, despite the high costs of servicing the current overdraft. The trust deeds restricted borrowing to one and a half times the aggregate of issued share capital plus the capital and revenue reserves. In now proposing to raise this limit by an additional third, the board offered to increase the interest payable to stock holders for a five-year period.[61]

A few weeks later, the search for a new managing director ended with the appointment of Peter Thrower, the assistant managing director of Rank Xerox. Explaining that the process had been so drawn out because it had not been easy to find an individual who combined the necessary business expertise with administrative skill and, above all, 'a vital quality of constructive leadership', Moray, albeit unconsciously, merely underlined his own shortcomings.[62] Thrower was soon joined by the other promised external appointee in the form of David Donne, a professional company director who had recently been involved with the financial restructuring of Cammell Laird. The new managing director's pruning knife proved to be both swift and sharp. Two English factories had already been axed by the time the Belfast plant went in January 1971, with the loss of 230 jobs. This was followed by the sale of the Minimodels premises at Havant and the closure of Shuresta in Coventry, with the loss of another 650 jobs. Altogether between December 1970 and August 1971, eight of Lines' twenty-four British factories were closed, while 1,700 employees – over a fifth of the UK workforce – were laid off between July 1970 and May 1971 alone.

This radical surgery was supplemented by a near twenty per cent price hike and a halving in the number of items produced, but the patient still appeared to be too far gone when, on 21 June 1971, Lines announced an accumulated loss for 1970 of £4,600,000. At this point Moray finally threw in the towel and resigned, with Darby replacing him in the chair. He faced a daunting task. More than £9,500,000 was owed to banks, over half of it to Lloyds, and with interest rates still high, the cost of this debt was crippling. Furthermore, at the end of 1970 the banks had stipulated that their continued financial backing was conditional on every part of the group providing a cross-guarantee for Lines Brothers. But then the prospects seemed to brighten when the tobacco giant, Gallaher, offered to inject £5,000,000 into the ailing business, a proposal contingent upon additional support from Hamleys. Notwithstanding the fact it had already borrowed £800,000 from Hamleys, the parent company consequently requested an additional loan to be raised by the sale and lease back of Hamleys' premises in Regent Street. Aware that if Lines Brothers went down the existing loan, which represented its own entire financial reserve, might be lost, the Hamleys' board went along with the suggestion, thereby raising £565,000 for the group, although reaching this decision was certainly eased by the fact that six of the seven-strong board were members of the Lines family.[63] But it was all in vain, for on 19 August the Gallaher offer was abruptly withdrawn. In part, this was because Lines' current trading position still showed no sign of improvement but it was also heavily influenced by the announcement, four days earlier, that the United States was unilaterally withdrawing from the Bretton Woods Accord. This postwar financial settlement had made for economic stability by pegging the dollar to the price of gold and other currencies to the dollar – effectively a system of fixed exchange rates. But now the American decision to allow the dollar to float (sterling followed suit shortly afterwards) created massive uncertainties about the basis of pricing in international trade, uncertainties to which Gallaher felt disinclined to expose its business. On receipt of the news from Gallaher, and under mounting pressure from creditors, the Lines board concluded that there remained no alternative but to recommend liquidation. It was agreed that Paul Shewell, a partner in Cooper Brothers, be appointed as liquidator and that a special meeting of interested parties be scheduled for 7 September to ratify this decision.

On 2 September, Hamleys received a phone call from the Lines group secretary, J. B. Hartley, outlining details of a scheme agreed with the banks. In return for the banks' continued financial support, the parent company and the subsidiaries which had provided the cross-guarantees were all to be liquidated. The latter's assets would then be hived off to new sub-subsidiary companies, thereby absolving them from liability for all existing debts. They would then be able to trade on a cash-only basis, subsequently creating debentures in favour of the banks for new borrowing.[64] When the special meeting summoned by the Lines board convened on 7 September, Shewell told the creditors that with the group's debt currently standing at £17,554,000, breaking it up would realise only £7,881,000, leaving them with only forty-four pence for every pound they were owed. He was even gloomier about the prospects for shareholders, who had also been invited to attend. The ordinary shares, he confirmed, were effectively worthless, and in fact they closed that day at a token three farthings. But some of the shareholders had not been convinced of the need to wind the business up anyway, and still cherished a hope that it might be sold as a going concern to a single purchaser. Moray, like his siblings still a shareholder despite his resignation, then rose to read out a telegram from no less a figure than Louis Marx, who was to the American toy industry what Walter Lines was to the British. It contained the news that the British toy conglomerate, Dunbee-Combex-Marx (DCM), had made an offer of £3,000,000. Like Marx, Moray knew that this was too small a sum to settle the banks, but it was, he suggested, evidence that with a little more time a suitable buyer might emerge. Graeme then added weight to this by suggesting that others were interested – years later he claimed that he had been talking to General Foods which was prepared to invest in Lines if he were to become chairman.[65] Peter Thrower certainly mentioned General Foods and also Nabisco as potential suitors. At this stage any straw, no matter how fragile, seemed worth grasping. The creditors agreed to establish an informal committee to work with the board and to take no immediate action against Lines, whereupon the meeting adjourned to allow for further discussions.

The next day, all dealings in Lines Brothers' shares were temporarily suspended while both Donne and Nicolson, the two directors most experienced in saving corporate invalids, promptly resigned. No reasons were given publicly, but there was clearly little meeting of minds between the hard-nosed professionals who had favoured liquidation in the belief that the group's prognosis was irredeemably terminal, and those shareholders whose motives in seeking a stay of execution certainly involved a degree of sentiment and sheer disbelief that a company such as Lines could actually go to the wall. It was also on 8 September that Peggy Lines told her board colleagues at Hamleys about a phone call received six days earlier from the group secretary, ordering her to comply with the liquidation scheme as outlined. Although she had wisely asked for written confirmation of this instruction, none had been received by the time she reported the matter to her board, indicative perhaps of the air of confusion and panic rapidly enveloping the organisation. Lines' executives were even told by their own accountants to withhold the true cash flow position from those advising Hamleys: subsidiaries were instructed not to adjust inter-company balances but to pass all credits to headquarters: Hamleys' general manager was probably not the only senior executive receiving commands and counter-commands on an almost daily basis, and he was even threatened with dismissal should he fail to trade in accordance with the diktats from head office.[66]

The reality was that it was something of a gamble and all too late. Although a couple of the group's businesses did duly comply by going into liquidation and then re-establishing themselves as sub-subsidiaries (Meccano became Meccano (1971) Ltd.: Tri-ang-Pedigree became Tri-ang-Pedigree Realisations Ltd.), the problems were so overwhelming and the network of interlocking financial commitments so complex that it was increasingly unrealistic to expect a single purchaser to step in and buy the whole operation, especially when it seemed likely that its various component businesses could soon be picked off separately: that at least was Peggy Lines' view.[67] The last lingering hopes of an external saviour evaporated on 17 September, when the DCM directors indicated that Lines needed a cash injection far greater than they had originally anticipated and that could not justify any increase in their offer. The banks, already dismayed by the delay agreed on 7 September, refused any further extension of funding and, by the time the adjourned

Lines' meeting reassembled on 28 September, the creditors, too, had lost patience, threatening to petition for a compulsory liquidation order. It was not necessary. By a majority of more than ten to one the shareholders' votes were cast in favour of voluntary liquidation. After more than half a century Lines Brothers had finally run out of road.

Chapter Six

In the Breaker's Yard

The collapse of Lines Brothers, responsible for about a fifth of total toy production in Britain, was a bombshell for the trade. It was seven years before the unsecured creditors, including those holding unsecured loan stock, were eventually paid off in full. Others with a personal financial stake in the business, including ordinary and preference shareholders, got nothing. Their response was understandably less measured than that of managing director Peter Thrower who commented rather laconically on the failure to find a purchaser that 'both time and money were against us – we just did not have time to get the company straight.'[1] 'The new board of super directors,' wrote two of Thrower's critics, 'has made an incredible mess during their short period in office, beside which the old Lines family Board *seem* far more efficient.'[2] But this hardly represented a ringing endorsement of the previous regime either, although it was certainly true that Lines' long-serving directors, drawn mainly from the family or the business itself, had a level of emotional and personal attachment to the company not shared by more recent outside recruits. More generally, the wide geographical scope of Lines' operations diluted the impact of its collapse on local employment and the company's demise, therefore, passed largely unremarked by the public at large, eclipsed by the spectacular failures earlier in the year of Rolls Royce and Upper Clyde Shipbuilders.[3] Furthermore, most of the group's component parts survived, eagerly snapped up by the circling predators. Indeed, the breaker's men were swift to cast a calculating eye over the wreckage, with over ninety inquiries made by late September. Within a year or two the process of demolition had been pretty well completed.[4]

Tube Investments paid £2,250,000 for Cyclops Tri-ang (Australia) and, via Raleigh, also bought the Canadian business in 1972. In the same year, Tri-ang-Pedigree in South Africa was acquired by Brick and Clay Holdings of Cape Town for £600,000. Closer to home, Combined English Stores paid £270,000 for the Youngsters chain, a shrewd purchase given that the shops' book value in early September stood at £528,000.[5] Lines' other retailing enterprise followed a different trajectory, however. As a partially owned subsidiary, Hamley Brothers had initially been placed in some difficulty by Lines' liquidation because its own outstanding accounts with suppliers were frozen. After some difficult discussions with Lloyds Bank, Peggy Lines secured a fresh overdraft facility allowing creditors to be paid and the famous store was able to continue trading, albeit as a new entity, Hamleys of Regent Street. Subsequently, she also retrieved most of what Hamleys had loaned the parent company, much to the satisfaction of her own minority shareholders.[6] As for the British-based manufacturing subsidiaries, DCM did now decide to invest, but only in the Rovex-Tri-ang division for which it paid £2,590,000, over £1,000,000 up front with a further £1,250,000 interest free and payable at the end of two years. A few months later in April 1972, the American toy makers Milton Bradley acquired the Lines' subsidiary, Arrow Games. Meccano went to Airfix for £2,700,000, £1,100,000 of which was deferred, interest free, until 31 December 1973. Hales' directors opted for a management buyout and purchased their own share capital from the liquidators. Pedigree was finally wound up in 1976 as was Unique and Unity, with declared assets of £93,500 and £4,500 respectively, claimable against Lines Brothers.

The iconic heart of the Lines empire, Tri-ang-Pedigree, went to Barclay Securities, a satellite of the notorious Slater-Walker group, which had already bought Chad Valley and the pressed steel toy maker Sebel and Co. to form the Barclay Toy Group in December 1971. The addition of Tri-ang (£3,600,000 for the share capital and £1,680,000 for the freehold of the Merton and Birmingham factories), made it the largest such organisation in Europe. Robert Upsdell, Barclay's managing director had been recruited from Slater-Walker and his callous culls of personnel and products, together with reviews of processes, prices and products had massively improved the sales and profits of the group's previous purchases and he certainly expected his latest acquisition to pay its way. In a thinly disguised dig at Lines' executives, he asserted that proper management working hard with no time off for midweek golf was effectively exposing the myth that toy making could not be made profitable.⁷ Yet Tri-ang apparently proved too daunting a challenge even for him, and within six months Barclay disposed of it because, Upsdell said, the overheads were simply too high to make it profitable.⁸ The Birmingham factory was sold on to Raleigh for £800,000 and the wooden toy business to Goodwood Playthings for £225,000. Even as negotiations got under way for the sale of the Lines' pram business, the Merton site went for £3,300,000 plus a share in a property investment company, giving a profit of some £2,400,000 on the properties alone. Twelve hundred workers at Merton were thrown onto the dole queues and John Bentley, Barclay Securities' chief executive, curtly dismissed an appeal from the local Conservative MP on the grounds that he could hardly be expected to keep a factory open simply for the benefit of employees. It was a logical enough retort but it seems highly unlikely that he ever had any genuine intention of turning Tri-ang around, for half a year was far too brief a period to deal with problems which a serious buyer would have carefully analysed before laying out over five million pounds. As he once told Graeme Lines, Bentley believed that 'any bloody fool can make money in the toy industry', but clearly that did not necessarily entail actually making any toys.⁹ He was, as *The Times* asserted, Britain's number one asset stripper, a judgement well merited by his speedy and ruthless disposal of Tri-ang.¹⁰

It was somewhat ironic that the day before this description of Bentley appeared in print, Walter Lines died. As Britain's most feared corporate predator and a millionaire by the time he was 28, Bentley viewed toys merely as commercial commodities, another means of making easy money by exploiting the achievements of others. Walter, on the other hand, was a toy maker first and a businessman second, a man for whom toys were primarily vehicles (literally so in the case of his pedal cars) for giving pleasure and enjoyment to children. He lived and breathed for his products, never happier than at his drawing board designing a new plaything and even in retirement setting up a small design studio in his garden to indulge his passion. In the words of one obituarist, he was 'not merely a manufacturer, he was a real toy maker.'¹¹ Of course, that passion had earned him substantial material rewards: his house at Leigh Place in Surrey had seven bedrooms, a billiard room, a study, four attic rooms and a staff flat. It stood in twenty-four acres of land which also contained a substantial lake, extensive stabling and a cottage. When it went on the market early in 1973 the asking price was £150,000 which, combined with the £86,000 or so he left in his will, gave him total assets worth about £3,100,000 in today's terms. The sale of the family home was a poignant symbol of the final dissolution of all that he and his brothers had built during his lifetime. Somehow, too, his very last words – 'somebody's stolen my socks' – seemed appropriately mundane for a man who had begun his working life by nailing cows' tails on to rocking horses.[12]

'The life cycle of a company ends,' remarked *The Times* in August 1971, 'either when there is no further demand for the products it makes or when the management ceases to be able to supply those products profitably.'[13] It is true that since Lines Brothers' establishment in 1919, the period over which children played with traditional toys became briefer, while the demand for large-wheeled toys, in which Lines at one time held three-quarters of the market, tended to stagnate as intensifying traffic volumes made streets less safe for children's play. In the light of such changes, it might plausibly be argued that failure to update the product lines more regularly and more thoroughly did contribute to Lines' difficulties. However, even if some toys did survive for too long and even if the company's output seemed to become less innovative and more imitative over time, bikes, dolls' prams, boats, train sets, dolls and soft toys possessed an enduring appeal, as did more recent products such as Sindy, Scalextric, Dinky, and even Meccano, hence the sale of £38,000,000 worth of goods in 1970. This was undoubtedly why major firms such as Gallaher, General Foods and DCM expressed interest in acquiring the whole enterprise – at least until the sheer magnitude of its financial problems became clear – and also why, after liquidation, its component parts were so swiftly gobbled up.

If then there is little to suggest that there was too much wrong with what Lines was actually making by 1971, and if *The Times'* analysis was correct, it follows that the company collapsed because it was unable to continue to supply all of its products profitably. Of course, things had moved on a good deal from the days when Walter had personally gone through each annual catalogue pencilling in suggested price changes, seemingly based on little more than whimsy. But the tighter trading environment of the later 1960s exposed crucial weaknesses in Lines' processes for controlling costs, and which required immediate redress as the consultants' 1970 report recognised. Their verdict was confirmed when Rovex-Tri-ang was taken over by DCM, its newly installed managing director identifying his primary task as putting 'some financial sense into the operation'.[14]

No comprehensive collection of Lines Brothers' business records remains, but the few surviving fragments and other sources do suggest a number of possible explanations for the group's deteriorating cost competitiveness. One common at the time was that the company's product range was too diverse, another consequence of the failure to prune the catalogue more regularly and ruthlessly. As one review of contemporary toy manufacturing put it, Lines Brothers had 'been for years competing in too many directions at once without apparently costing at all. In fact, unchecked costs have pushed the company's breakeven point too high without any apparent control.'[15] Of course there is some merit in the counter argument that diversity actually provided some protection against market volatility: after all, Lesney, essentially a one-product business, suffered heavy losses and took some time to recover after Hot Wheels bit so deeply into sales of its Matchbox toys. But at Lines Brothers diversification does not seem to have been accompanied by much standardisation of processes or components: across the group as a whole, for example, no fewer than 137 different types of rivet and 147 different formers for bending metal tubes were in use in the 1960s. Opportunities for other production economies were lost or delayed by the tardiness with which plant was written off, replaced, or utilised. Meccano proved a particular burden in this respect: in the inquests which inevitably followed Lines' collapse, some even suggested that its primary cause was the failure to grapple with Meccano's cost inefficiencies. J. G. Thomas, who as Meccano's long-serving assistant company secretary was in a good position to know, certainly took this view. He recalled instances of brand-new plant left lying idle at Binns Road because management had failed to agree its deployment with the unions.[16] Consequently, sales were often lost because the factory failed to deliver the required volumes of production levels in time.

Labour relations at Meccano may have proved particularly difficult for Lines and there were also issues with a communist-dominated work force in the Lyons factory, but otherwise there was little evidence of trade union militancy, and relationships between employer and employed generally remained harmonious, as a little vignette from the 1940s illustrates. Until he was replaced by Moray, Walter served on the Toy Trade Board and its postwar successor the Toy Manufacturing Wages Council, both statutorily responsible for determining wages in the industry, although from the very outset his own firm always paid more than the industry average or the officially prescribed rates. He was thus embarrassed and annoyed when, in October 1947, the Wages Council received a letter from the shop stewards at Merton deploring its latest pay proposals as unrealistic. He promptly produced a supplementary communication from his workers making it clear that they had written in solidarity with employees in the industry as a whole, not on their own behalf, since they were satisfied with their own levels of pay.[17]

But if the group's difficulties owed little to trade union militancy – what Europeans would ultimately refer to as the 'British disease' – labour issues did contribute to failing cost competitiveness in another way, in that general wage inflation reached seven or eight per cent by the end of the 1960s. This of course affected all manufacturers equally but in Lines' case it was exacerbated by the fact that its overheads had been allowed to get out of hand. Whatever their initial intentions had been with respect to Tri-ang, Bentley and Upsdell did have a point when they stressed that it could not be made to pay when overheads were so high.[18] Nor was Tri-ang the only part of the group saddled with excessive overheads, as Table 10 illustrates. It provides a proxy overhead measurement in the form of a calculation of the ratio between productive and non-productive labour in the various factories and subsidiaries towards the end of the 1960s. Some units were clearly operating efficiently and even showing signs of improvement, but

Table 10. Lines Brothers Ltd. Ratio of Non-productive to Productive Wages 1967–1968 (%)

Operation	1967	1968
Merthyr	98.95	98.98
Birmingham	52.34	50.63
Mini-Models	40.96	50.81
Meccano	244.99	235.29
Good-Wood	34.39	28.65
Rovex	107.8	104.5
Pedigree Merton	80.98	100.16
Pedigree Belfast	109.4	106.8
Pedigree Richmond	78.39	68.91

Source: MOC. P. Lines Archive. Uncatalogued. Memo headed 'Calculation of % of non-productive wages to productive wages'.

at Rovex, Merthyr and Belfast the adverse ratio was unacceptably high, while the lack of any overall control and the failure to secure improvement in this direction allowed performance at Minimodels and Merton to deteriorate over the measured twelve-month period. Worst of all was Meccano, where expenditure on non-productive staff remained almost two and a half times higher than that attributable to workers on the factory floor. Graeme Lines certainly recognised this problem but was unable to uproot the culture on which it rested, and which ultimately would also bring about the downfall of its new owners, Airfix.

Table 10 also suggests a third explanation for Lines' failing competitiveness, for it reveals the wide geographical spread of production within Britain, a feature mirrored in the far-flung overseas manufacturing locations established since 1945. At home, physical dispersion was a consequence of the rather haphazard way in which the business had been expanded over the decades, often it has to be reiterated in response to outside approaches – in the cases of IMA, Pedigree and Wrenn for instance – rather than as the implementation of any agreed strategic plan. It could equally be said that the decision to locate production facilities in Wales and Northern Ireland was also the result of external forces, first in that permission for postwar expansion at Merton was denied by government, and second in that the official incentives offered to establish new plants outside the south of England proved attractive at a time when sales were relatively easy. However, by the early 1960s transport costs as a percentage of product selling prices were two per cent higher for goods made in Merthyr and Belfast than for those made elsewhere. The latter's geographical vulnerability was further highlighted in 1966 when a seamen's strike deprived the plant of raw materials, leaving warehouses full of stock which could not be shipped out, and half the workforce temporarily laid off. Such drawbacks probably explain why in the 1960s Lines rejected further government blandishments to set up additional plants in designated development areas.[19] It may be, too, that the board was becoming aware that continuous expansion carried with it the risk of diluting the sense of corporate pride and identity so consciously cultivated in the early days, a danger which perhaps lay behind the decisions to launch the in-house magazine *Leading Lines* in the early 1960s, and also to re-emphasise the Tri-ang brand.

As for the overseas plants, the emphasis on establishing manufacturing capabilities inside national tariff barriers, whether imperial or European, was a logical course to pursue in the postwar years given the persistence of international protectionism, but Richard Lines for one thought that his uncle's investment choices were sometimes more of a penchant as often based on whim as on any sound economic rationale.[20] The Canadian business certainly struggled for a long time while the several acquisitions in France were widely spread geographically, and Lyons, in particular, proved disastrous with managers struggling to work with a highly unionised and communist-influenced labour force.

Physical dispersion, rising wages, high overheads, production inefficiencies and (arguably) too wide a range of outputs, all played a part in reducing Lines' competitiveness and bringing the group down in 1971. It is possible that the difficulties might have been discerned and addressed more promptly had expansion over the years been accompanied by any significant structural reorganisation of the sort which, it has been suggested, made American big business in particular so robust and competitive. In the United States, this argument runs, diversified businesses evolved multi-divisional structures each operating autonomously under their own management, but with corporate strategy, resource allocation and overall performance all determined and monitored by a single overarching central body. In such a structure, effective co-ordination depended on the development of sophisticated control systems.[21] The proposition that this type of corporate organisation was competitively superior has been much contested, with studies of German and Japanese business, for example, indicating that more traditional family-owned enterprises were not inherently disadvantaged by their failure to develop more modern structures.[22] But whatever the general validity of these various hypotheses, as far as Lines Brothers is concerned, the consultants' report did certainly place great emphasis on the lack of any effective system of central oversight, particularly with respect to cost control and strategic planning, which may have enabled it to weather the storm of the early 1970s. But three decades of favourable trading conditions had fostered a high degree of complacency, as one leading trade journal implied: 'There is something genuinely sad about the demise of a British institution, sad not because of the decline itself but because of the institution's feeling that it was indestructible, that it should have been allowed to survive.'[23] Graeme Lines virtually acknowledged this when he conceded, in the face of the challenge from Mattel, that Lines had been content for too long to trade on its name and reputation.

In turn, Lines' failure to develop more appropriate and robust management systems may reflect a specific feature of British family-owned businesses and which distinguished them from their international peers – a reluctance to hire significant numbers of professional managers.[24] Outside investors, both institutional and private, may have come to hold more of the equity during the postwar decades, but the Lines group, like many contemporary British manufacturing enterprises, was essentially a traditional holding company with overall control vested firmly in the family hands. New acquisitions were usually run by a reconfigured board chaired by a member of the parent company board, meaning that overall responsibility and direction for what ultimately became a large-scale international enterprise rested on only a handful of people.

Furthermore, because most of these individuals tended to be recruited either from long-serving employees or from within the immediate family circle, the consequence was an over-reliance on executives with little significant outside experience, and who for the most part lacked a broad grasp of general management principles, having worked only in a single part of the business or possessing expertise only in a particular aspect of it. Richard Lines, for instance, spent most of his career with Rovex while Peter's roles as company secretary in Canada and at Pedigree limited his expertise primarily to matters of legal and financial regulation. Graeme specialised in sales and marketing: it was no coincidence that shortly after Lines' demise, he was promoting a new sales gimmick for toys based on the same principle as book tokens. As the management consultants concluded in 1970, this reluctance – until it was too late – to recruit top professional executives from outside the group left Lines dangerously short in vital areas, especially financial control, strategic planning, and marketing, a prime consequence being the massive miscalculation on projected sales in 1969. Barclays' Robert Upsdell shared their diagnosis and clearly had Lines in mind when he told an interviewer that, in the past, toy manufacturers had rarely emphasised strong management, prospering almost in spite of themselves.[25] Gerald Lucas's criticism of Lines in 1970 may have been sparked by his exasperation as a retailer with specific inefficiencies in the accounts and sales departments, but he also dismissed the entire Lines management as 'bad'. He further suggested that even if the Americans retreated from the British market, they would leave behind a legacy of professionalism that would never be lost even though it had not previously been apparent among British producers.[26] In similar vein, Basil Feldman, DCM's managing director, suggested that while Lines' last desperate efforts at rationalisation were exactly what was needed, they failed because 'management simply wasn't up to it'.[27] Local bosses certainly thought the decision to close Shuresta as part of the restructuring process was an instance of the parent company's capacity for mismanagement, since it was made without any prior consultation and in spite of a full order book.[28]

Ultimately of course, the buck stopped at the top. Walter Lines and his brothers had set up their business – largely on borrowed capital – at a time when the economic prospects were volatile and uncertain, and they subsequently carried it to prosperity despite the difficulties of a global depression and a second world war. They can hardly be held to account for the fact that the structure and organisation, which allowed their business to flourish, proved insufficiently robust to withstand subsequent changes in the trading environment, although there were some who suggested that the response might have been swifter and more effective had Walter's active involvement and influence, in particular, not lasted so long. This seems too harsh, but there was certainly some truth in the observation of a trade journalist that 'until their very fall there was always something unrealistically "family" paternal about the company.'[29] Nor can the brothers be faulted for wishing to pass the business on to their children, but Moray who like his siblings had worked his way up through the company and inevitably absorbed its culture, certainly did not drive the company as his father had done. In the face of difficulty, he seemed to flounder, offering little more than ill-founded rhetoric and little in the way of strategic leadership: it was no mere exercise in window dressing when the consultants' recommended that his successor as managing director should be recruited from outside the company. Nor was Moray much helped by a board whose challenge function seems to have been somewhat blunted not only by complacency but also by a reticence to speak frankly, a reluctance born of long-standing friendships and blood ties. So bad had things become by 1970 that neither Thrower, nor a more professional board purged of most of the Lines family, proved able to save the company, although by then time and the burden of debt were heavily against them.

It is worth stressing, in conclusion, that the weaknesses which made the Lines Brothers group vulnerable were by no means unique. In fact, they were endemic across vast swathes of contemporary British manufacturing industry, as was to become all too apparent under the free market regime championed by the Conservative administrations of Margaret Thatcher after 1979, which saw wholesale bankruptcies and failures. Lines may have gone down in 1971, but as far as British toy making was concerned, its fate was a mere harbinger of what was to come. Between 1979 and 1983, the heart was torn out of the industry by a sequence of dissolutions which swept away virtually all the dominant companies of the postwar years including Airfix, DCM, Meccano, Lesney, Mettoy, Lone Star, and Malins.[30] But this simply serves to underline the oft-overlooked reality that, historically, most business enterprises eventually fail and that long-lived concerns are the exceptions rather than the rule. Perhaps the more interesting aspect of Lines Brothers' history, therefore, lies not so much in the explanation of its final collapse but rather in its successful development from a second-hand woodwork factory to arguably the world's largest and first multinational toy company. Those fond of determinist explanations of history, whether couched in economic, geographic, biological or even climatic terms, generally underestimate the role of the individual in past events. But in 1972 Alan Hancock, a relative newcomer to toy manufacturing, shrewdly observed that the British industry had been built by a few individuals with the flair to see and take advantage of business opportunities.[31] Unconsciously or otherwise, he was echoing elements of Joseph Schumpeter's classic definition of entrepreneurship. Hancock's caveat, that success had been more usually a matter of luck than judgement, certainly cannot be discounted entirely as far as Lines Brothers is concerned, but it should not be allowed to detract from the talents, energy and vision which Walter, in particular, but more than ably abetted by Arthur and Will, brought to British toy making over four decades. The business they built may long since have vanished but the underlying conviction on which it rested, that toys were not merely commercial commodities from which to make money but playthings to delight, educate and amuse children, should stand as a worthy memorial to three remarkable individuals.

Notes

Chapter One: Learners: Fathers and Sons, 1850–1918

1. Fourth Report from the select committee on artisans and machinery, British Parliamentary Papers, V (1824), p. 314. Osler's sons went on to build their father's business so successfully that it survived until 1965.
2. G. C. Bartley, 'Toys' in G. P. Bevan ed., *British Manufacturing Industries* (1876), p. 154
3. T. South, *Discourse on the Common Weal of this Realm of England* (1549). Quoted in J. Thirsk, *Economic Policy and Projects: the Development of a Consumer Society in Early Modern England* (1978), p. 14
4. H. & L. Mui, *Shops and Shopkeeping in Eighteenth-Century England* (1989), p. 69
5. J. Austen, *Northanger Abbey* (1803), p. 1
6. M. & R. L. Edgeworth, *Essay on Practical Education* (1812), p. 46
7. M. Braddon, *Lady Audley's Secret* (Oxford reprint, 2012), pp. 149, 273, 317, 225
8. Figures for the numbers of London shops over the period are in D. Alexander, *Retailing in England During the Industrial Revolution* (1970), pp. 239-55
9. *Punch, or the London Charivari*, 11 (1846), p. 96
10. K. D. Brown, *The British Toy Business: A History Since 1700* (1996), pp. 22, 46
11. J. R. McCulloch, *A Dictionary, Practical, Theoretical, and Historical of Commerce and Commercial Navigation* (1835), p. 1168
12. *Morning Chronicle*, 21 February 1850
13. *Ibid.*, 28 February 1850
14. *Ibid.*, 21 February 1850
15. *Ibid.*, 28 February 1850
16. London Metropolitan Archives. MS 11936/553/122283, Sun Fire Office.

17. *Business Directory of London* (1864), pp. 668-9
18. L. Levi, *Wages and Earnings of the Working Classes* (1867), p. 54
19. C. Dickens, *The Cricket on the Hearth* (1846)
20. *Morning Chronicle*, 21 February 1850
21. *Ibid.*, 28 February 1850
22. Great Exhibition of 1851. *Reports of the Juries and Royal Commissioners* (1852), p. 1521
23. *Morning Chronicle*, 21 February 1850
24. *Ibid.*
25. *Ibid.*, 28 February 1850
26. Dickens, *The Cricket*, p. 60
27. Great Exhibition of 1851, *Reports*, p. 1519
28. E. E. Nesbit, *Wings and the Child* (1913), p. 38
29. G. Sala, *Notes and Sketches of the Paris Exhibition* (1867), p. 151
30. W. H. Cremer, *The Toys of the Little Folks* (1873), pp. 45-9
31. Bartley, 'Toys', p. 154
32. N. F. R. Crafts, 'Economic Growth in France and Britain, 1830–1914: A Review of the Evidence', *Journal of Economic History*, 44 (1984), p. 54
33. For an excellent survey see J. Benson, *The Rise of Consumer Society in Britain 1880–1980* (1994), pp. 1-55
34. J. Hollingshead, *Ragged London in 1861* (1986 reprint), p. 23
35. M. Pember Reeves, *Round About a Pound a Week* (1913), p. 192
36. B. S. Rowntree and M. Kendall, *How the Labourer Lives: A Study of the Rural Labour Problem* (1913), p. 312
37. T. Thompson, *Edwardian Childhoods* (1981), p. 222
38. H. Cunningham, *Children of the Poor: Representations of Childhood Since the Seventeenth Century* (Oxford, 1991), p. 35
39. *Graphic*, 16 December 1871
40. Bartley, 'Toys', p. 200. My italics.
41. *The Times*, 21 April 1908
42. *Fancy Goods and Toy Trades Journal*, 9 March 1891. The identical point was made in *Games, Toys and Amusements* (May 1895), p. 34
43. *Porter's Topographical and Commercial Directory of Leeds* (1872–3); *Robinson's Directory of Leeds* (1901); *Slater's Directory of Manchester*

and *Salford* (1876, 1901); *Ward's Directory of Newcastle, Gateshead etc* (1865–6, 1900)
44. E. E. Williams, *Made in Germany* (1896). For a critical discussion of his claims see Brown, *British Toy Business*, pp. 66–8
45. W. Lines, *Looking Backwards and Looking Forwards* (1958), p. 7
46. *Athletic Sports, Games and Toys* (March 1896), p. 20
47. E. Farjeon, *A Nursery in the Nineties* (1935), p. 312
48. National Archives (NA). BT 55/80/88. Minutes of proceedings before the committee appointed under the Safeguarding of Industries Act 1921 to consider complaints with regard to toys. 17 February 1922
49. C. Feinstein, 'New estimates of average earnings in the United Kingdom, 1880–1913', *Economic History Review*, 43 (1990), pp. 603–4
50. M. Heller, 'London Clerical Workers 1880–194: The Search for Stability', University of London PhD (2003), pp. 70–1
51. NA. BT 55/80/88. Minutes of proceedings before the committee appointed under the Safeguarding of Industries Act 1921 to consider complaints with regard to toys, 17 February 1922
52. Museum of Childhood (MOC). Peggy Lines Archive. Uncatalogued. G. & J. Lines. Turnover and Net Profit, 1912–1918
53. Quoted in P. Lines, *From G & J to Tri-ang: The Lines Family Toy Businesses The First 80 Years* (2015), p. 34
54. J. Lines to M. Lines, n.d. Cited in *ibid.*, p. 22
55. George did well out of his toy making, however, for when he died in 1922 he left £7,662, the equivalent of about £378,000 today. *The Times*, 16 March 1922
56. MOC. P. Lines Archive. Uncatalogued. J. Lines to A. Lines, 14 August 1909
57. Lines, *Looking Backwards*, p. 8
58. J. Lines to M. Lines, n.d. Quoted in Lines, *G & J to Tri-ang*, p. 22
59. This comment was contained in an interview given years later. *Financial Times*, 20 November 1961
60. Quoted in Lines, *G & J to Tri-ang*, p. 46
61. Quoted in *ibid.*
62. Jane Lines to W. Lines, 16 March 1914. Quoted in *ibid.*
63. J. Wilson, *British Business History, 1720–1994* (Manchester, 1995), p. 111

64. Quoted in Lines, *G & J to Tri-ang*, p. 59
65. For Meccano see K. D. Brown, *Factory of Dreams: A History of Meccano Limited, 1901–1979* (Lancaster, 2007) p. 36. The Bassett-Lowke figure is cited in R. Fuller, *The Bassett-Lowke Story* (1985), p. 27. The other figures are from NA. BT 55/80/88. Minutes of proceedings before the committee appointed under the Safeguarding of Industries Act 1921 to consider complaints with regard to toys, 5 February–2 March 1922
66. *The Times*, 7 September 1914
67. *Ibid.*, 13 May 1915
68. *Toy and Fancy Goods Trader*, 15 February 1916
69. NA. BT 54/18/1. Board of Trade. British Industries Fair.
70. NA. BT 55/80/87. Application under part II of the Safeguarding of Industries Act by the Incorporated Association of British Toy Manufacturers and Wholesalers Ltd. Report of a Departmental Committee of the Board of Trade. Summary, p. 31
71. MOC. P. Lines Archive. Uncatalogued. Sole, Tavernor & Knight to W. Lines, 25 November 1919
72. Lines, *Looking Backwards*, p. 10

Chapter Two: Going Solo, 1918–1929

1. Sir Auckland Geddes in reply to a trade delegation and reported in *Toyshop and Fancy Goods Journal* (September 1919), p. 94
2. MOC. P. Lines Archive. Uncatalogued. W. Lines Memo 'Factories and showrooms', 14 April 1971
3. Quoted in Lines, *G & J to Tri-ang*, p. 65
4. MOC. P. Lines Archive. Uncatalogued. R. Freeman to W. Lines, 15 March 1918
5. *Toyshop and Fancy Goods Journal*, 20 July 1917
6. The interview was cited in *ibid.*, 5 February 1918
7. This subject is discussed in F. Capie and G. Wood, 'Money in the Economy, 1870–1939', in R. Floud and D. McCloskey eds., *The Economic History of Britain Since 1700. Vol 2. 1860–1939* (Cambridge, second ed., 1995), pp. 217-46
8. Author's interview with Graeme Lines, 10 April 1991

Notes 159

9. Quoted in Lines, *G & J to Tri-ang*, p. 68
10. Our story: Start Bay Bungalows, startbaybungalows.co.uk
11. MOC. P. Lines archive. Uncatalogued. S. Carson to W. Lines, 22 March 1919
12. NA. LAB 2/482/TB10103/32/1919. Trade Boards. Summary report on the present position of the toy trade, 1919
13. Quoted in Lines, *G & J to Tri-ang*, p. 85
14. Quoted *in ibid.*, p. 67
15. MOC. P. Lines Archive. Uncatalogued. Price List, 1 August 1919
16. *Ibid.* Price List, 16 July 1919
17. MOC. Lines Brothers Archive. LINE 3/4/1. *British Standard Exporter* c. 1920
18. Quoted in Lines, *G & J to Tri-ang*, p. 68
19. Quoted in *ibid.*, p. 74
20. MOC. P. Lines Archive. Uncatalogued. Cyclostyled copy of the chairman's report for the fourteen months ending 30 June 1920
21. See, for example, comments in *Toy and Fancy Goods Journal*, 15 January 1917
22. *Games and Toys* (August 1923), p. 246
23. This at least was the view of the *Toy Trader* (April 1924), p. 72
24. MOC. P. Lines Archive. Uncatalogued. Printed page headed 'Lines Brothers Ltd.' and extracted from an unknown international trade directory.
25. For Hornby's approach to advertising see Brown, *Factory of Dreams*, pp. 70-75
26. MOC. P. Lines Archive. Uncatalogued. Handwritten poem in Joseph's hand.
27. *The Times*, 12 March 1918
28. NA. BT 55/80. Board of Trade. Safeguarding of Industries Committee on Toys. Minutes of Evidence, 5 February 1922, pp. 27, 36, 51
29. This is discussed at some length in Brown, *British Toy Business*, pp. 106-9
30. As reported in *Toyshop and Fancy Goods Journal* (September 1920), p. 29
31. *The Times*, 24 February 1921
32. NA. BT 55/80/87. Application under Part II of the Safeguarding of Industries Act by the Incorporated Association of British Toy

Manufacturers and Wholesalers Ltd. Report of a Departmental Committee of the Board of Trade, p. 3
33. NA. BT 55/80. Board of Trade. Safeguarding of Industries Committee on Toys. Minutes of Evidence, 17 February 1922
34. *Toy Trader* (October 1923), p. 24
35. *Ibid.* (December 1925), p. 20
36. MOC. P. Lines Archive. Uncatalogued. Paper headed 'Some of the reasons for the new factory'
37. NA. LAB 2/906/TB135/10/24. Report of an investigation into the overlap between the toy trade and the perambulator trade, 1924/5, p. 18
38. *Ibid.*, p. 58
39. NA. LAB 2/482/TB10103/32/1919. Trade Boards. Summary report on the present position of the toy trade (1919)
40. NA. LAB 41/250. Information relating to the toy manufacturing trade (1927)
41. See W. H. Nicholls, *Toy-Making in Liverpool: The Most Important Centre in the Country* (Liverpool, 1919): *Overseas Buyers' Guide to British Toys and Fancy Goods* (1919) pp. 60 ff: K. D. Brown, 'An Absorbing Epic? The Development of Toy Manufacturing in the North West, c.1851–1931', *Manchester Region History Review*, 21 (2010), pp. 87-103
42. NA. LAB 11/2407. Information relating to sundry trade board industries. Toy making, 1927
43. *Toy Trader* (May 1927), p. 44
44. *Ibid.* (September 1927), p. 62
45. NA. BT 31/45817. Board of Trade Companies Registration Office. Files of dissolved companies. No of Company 39827. Unique and Unity Cycle Company Ltd.
46. Even in 1935 one Portuguese visitor to the BIF was still complaining that too many British toy firms were ignorant of the metric system and his country's currency while instructions were too often provided only in English.
47. MOC. P. Lines Archive. Uncatalogued. Lines Brothers. Typescript draft of chairman's report for the 1928 AGM
48. A. D. Chandler, *Scale and Scope: the Dynamics of Industrial Capitalism* (Cambridge Mass., 1990), p. 8

49. L. Hannah, 'Takeover bids in Britain before 1950: an exercise in "prehistory"', *Business History*, XVI (1974), cited in J. Wilson, *British Business History, 1720–1994* (Manchester, 1995), p. 150
50. MOC. Lines Brothers Archive. LINE 3/1/13. Pedigree Pram Catalogue, 1927–8
51. MOC. P. Lines Archive. Uncatalogued. Lines Brothers. J. Rae to W. Lines, 19 February, 1929. There is no mention in this letter of the actual award Walter had been offered, but a civil service memo written thirty years later notes that it was a CBE which had been rejected because Walter thought he merited a knighthood. NA. BT 258/1382. Correspondence with Lines Brothers. Memo by J. L. May, 18 February 1960

Chapter Three: Rough Roads, 1929–1945

1. *Toy Trader* (April 1930), p 10: *ibid.*, (May 1930), p. 91
2. *Ibid.* (June 1931), p. 18
3. Brown, *British Toy Business*, p. 129
4. Author's interview with G. Lines, 10 April 1991
5. Robinson's claim was reported in *British Toys* (July 1973), p. 9. For the Meccano letter see Merseyside Maritime Museum (MMM). Meccano Archive. B/ME/20. Meccano to Daimler Co Ltd., 11 October 1934
6. *Toy Trader* (July 1931), p. 8
7. Author's interview with G. Lines, 10 April 1991
8. NA. BT 215/1291. Merchandise Marks Standing Committee. Papers. Toys and requisites for sports and games. Enquiry minutes, 12 January 1932
9. MOC. P. Lines Archive. Uncatalogued. Draft letter to Hamleys shareholders, 1933
10. Lines *Looking Backwards*, p. 30
11. In a letter to Peggy Lines quoted in Lines, *G & J to Tri-ang*, p. 153
12. MOC. P. Lines Archive. Uncatalogued. Hamley Bros Ltd. Third AGM, 7 May 1934
13. *Ibid.* Hamley Bros Ltd. Sixth AGM, 14 April 1937
14. *Ibid.* W. Lines to R. W. Dullam, 17 March 1933

15. *Ibid.* Lines Brothers Ltd. Letter to representatives, 14 April 1930
16. *Ibid.* Note to representatives and retailers, 19 June 1930
17. *Ibid.* Handwritten note, Catalogue 1930–3
18. *Ibid.* Letter fragment, unsigned and undated.
19. *Toy Trader* (March 1936), p. 26
20. MOC. P. Lines Archive. Uncatalogued. W. Lines to Mrs Smiles, 22 December 1932
21. *The Times*, 27 February 1936
22. *Toy Trader* (October 1931), p. 12
23. *Games & Toys* (November 1931), p. 34
24. *The Times*, 22 December 1933
25. *Toy Trader* (April 1934), p. 4
26. MOC. P. Lines Archive. Uncatalogued. W. Lines to Messrs. Walt Disney Mickey Mouse Ltd., 11 February 1936
27. *Toy Trader* (March 1934), p. 66
28. MOC. P. Lines Archive. Uncatalogued. G. Inglis to W. Lines, 17 December 1935
29. Lines, *Looking Backwards*, p. 25
30. This is derived from P. Van Lune, *FROG 'Penguin': Plastic Scale Model Kits 1936–1950* (Privately published. Vianen, 2017), pp. 10-16
31. For an alternative explanation of the derivation of FROG see *ibid.*, p. 16
32. MOC. P. Lines Archive. Uncatalogued. W. Lines to J. Rae, 22 December 1939
33. *Flight Magazine*, 10 November 1932
34. MOC. P. Lines Archive. Uncatalogued. Typed note headed 'Lines Brothers (Company)', dated later by Peggy Lines as May 1932
35. Lines, *G & J to Tri-ang*, p. 165
36. Quoted in Lune, *FROG 'Penguin'*, p. 56
37. Figures from J. G. Walshe, 'Industrial organisation and competition policy' in N. F. R. Crafts & N. Woodward eds., *The British Economy Since 1945* (Oxford, 1991), p. 337. Doubtless this was why the company was approached in 1936 to see if it would consider setting up an operation in one of the country's unemployment blackspots, officially designated as special or distressed areas. See MOC. P. Lines Archive. Uncatalogued. C. N. Ryan to J. Rae, 30 April 1936

Notes   163

38. See generally Chandler, *Scale and Scope*
39. MOC. British toy-making project. Mr W. Graeme Lines (August 2013), p. 8
40. MOC. P. Lines Archive. Uncatalogued. Aide-Mémoire, undated.
41. MOC. Lines Brothers Archive. LINE 3/1/39. W. J. Lines to Mr Brockbank, 10 March 1937
42. *Ibid*. W. J. Lines to Mr Matthews, 4 March 1937
43. MOC. P. Lines Archive. Uncatalogued. Memo re rush orders, 31 December 1935
44. An incident recounted by Salter in a letter of condolence sent when Will died. *Ibid*. P. Salter to R. Lines 23 April 1963
45. Lines, *Looking Backwards*, p. 30
46. MOC. P. Lines Archive. Uncatalogued. W. Lines to K. Barrington-Smith, 2 February 1936
47. Quoted in Lines, *G & J to Tri-ang*, p. 143
48. MOC. P. Lines Archive. W. Lines to G. Lines, 10 January 1936
49. *Ibid*. W. Lines to Mr Woollen, 1 April 1936
50. *Ibid*. R. Turner to W. Lines, 31 July 1931
51. *Financial Times*, 30 June 1936
52. These details are from NA. BT 31/45829. Board of Trade. Companies Registration Office. No. of Company 314841. Pedigree Soft Toys Limited.
53. *The Times*, 17 November 1937
54. MOC. P. Lines Archive. Uncatalogued. Note to dealers, 27 May 1937
55. *Financial Times*, 23 September 1938
56. *Toy Trader* (October 1939), p. 16
57. MOC. P. Lines Archive. Uncatalogued. Letter to customers from Pedigree Soft Toys, 7 September 1939
58. *Ibid*. W. Lines to J. Rae, 22 December 1939
59. *The Times*, 25 July 1940
60. *Ibid*., 27 July 1940
61. *Illustrated London News*, 3 August 1940
62. *The Times*, 24 October 1940
63. The note is reproduced in Lune, *FROG 'Penguin'*, p. 104
64. MOC. P. Lines Archive. Uncatalogued. W. Lines to D. Reader, 30 November 1943
65. *Ibid*. W. Lines to J. Rae, 22 December 1939

66. *The Times*, 18 December 1945
67. See generally D. Haunton, 'Lines Brothers' wartime pilotless aircraft', *Merton Historical Society Bulletin*, 163 (2007), pp. 6-9
68. NA. HO 192/1524. Ministry of Home Security. Research and Experiments Department, registered papers. Machine tools. High explosive damage, Lines Bros., Merton. 18/19 February 1944

Chapter Four: The Highway, 1945–1961

1. NA. BT 177/1131. Board of Trade. Distribution of Industry and Regional Division. Registered files. Lines Bros, Cyfarthfa. W. Lines to Ministry of Supply, 18 January 1944, and W. Lines to J. K. Peppercorn, 25 January 1944
2. *Ibid.* W. Lines to J. K. Peppercorn, 11 October 1944
3. NA. LAB 11/1799. Department of Employment and Predecessors. Industrial Relations, Trade Boards and Wages Council files. Toy Manufacturing Trade Board meeting, 31 October 1944
4. *Toy Trader and Exporter* (September 1947), p. 52
5. See, for example, *ibid.* (October 1949), p. 84
6. A. J. Wells of Wells-Brimtoy Ltd., cited in *The Times*, 19 July 1948
7. British Toy Manufacturers Association (BTMA), *Annual Report* (1945), n.p. The old Association of British Toy Manufacturers and Wholesalers had been defunct for several years before it was formally dissolved by notice in the *London Gazette*, 13 December 1932, leaving the manufacturers free to establish their own exclusive organisation. See NA. BT 31/22987/141603. Board of Trade. Companies Registration Office. Company No 141603. Solicitor's letter to Board of Trade, 12 May 1931
8. *The Times*, 26 September, 12 and 26 October, 9 and 23 November, 21 December 1945
9. Lines, *Looking Backwards*, p. 38
10. *The Times*, 21 December 1944
11. NA. BT 177/1131. Board of Trade. Distribution of Industry and Regional Division. Registered Files. Lines Bros., Cyfarthfa. Minute of meeting, 14 June 1945

12. *Ibid.*, W. Lines to P. Warter, 24 September 1945
13. *Ibid.*, W. Lines to J. K. Peppercorn, 24 October 1945
14. It was reported in 1952 that the company's entire design and development department was engaged in defence work arising from the Korean War. *Toy Trader and Exporter* (March 1952), p. 84
15. NA. BT 177/1132. Board of Trade. Distribution of Industry and Regional Division. Registered files. Lines Bros., Cyfarthfa
16. NA. BT 177/1131. Board of Trade. Distribution of Industry and Regional Division. Registered files. Lines Bros., Cyfarthfa. W. Lines to J. K. Peppercorn, 11 September 1945
17. Later interview on behalf of the Northern Ireland Development Council with Walter Lines and reported in *The Times*, 2 May 1956
18. *Ibid.*, 18 December 1945
19. *Ibid.*, 25 November 1947
20. *Ibid.*, 30 January 1947
21. *Ibid.*, 15 January 1949
22. *Ibid.*, 9 January 1951. Marx laid off 350 in Swansea for the same reason.
23. NA. BT 258/1382. Toy Manufacturers. Correspondence with Lines Brothers. W. Lines to Board of Trade, 11 March 1953
24. *Toy Trader and Exporter* (February 1951), p. 96
25. NA. BT 94/210. Board of Trade. Consumer Needs Department. Survey of the Toy Trade, 1951
26. *Ibid.*
27. The information and figures in this paragraph are drawn from various documents contained in NA. BT 64/4039. Board of Trade. Industries and Manufactures Department. Correspondence and Papers. Use of timber for manufacture of Toys & Fancy Goods Export Group. Memoranda and minutes.
28. *Toy Trader and Exporter* (December 1947), p. 34
29. This was the explanation later set out by Walter's son, Moray. See NA. BT 258/1383. Toy Manufacturers. Correspondence with Lines Brothers Ltd. W. M. Lines to G. Brown, 21 April 1965
30. In part, this explains why historically the bulk of British exports – almost forty-seven per cent in the 1930s – went to imperial territories.

See A. Marrison, *British Business and Protection, 1903–1932* (Oxford, 1996), p. 20
31. See generally D. Veart, *Hello Girls and Boys! A New Zealand Toy Story* (Auckland, 2014)
32. *The Times*, 15 January 1949
33. NA. BT 94/210. Board of Trade. Consumer Needs Department. Survey of the Toy Trade, 1951
34. *The Times*, 15 December 1952
35. *Ibid.*, 18 November 1952
36. *Economist*, 28 December 1957
37. *The Times*, 14 January 1950. Louis Marx and Company was probably larger and certainly had at least an equal claim to be the world's first multinational toy manufacturer since by 1951 it had a dozen factories worldwide, and four years later made the front cover of *Time Magazine*.
38. *Games and Toys* (August 1950), pp. 70-81
39. NA. BT 258/1382. Toy Manufacturers. Correspondence with Lines Brothers Ltd. American sales drive, 1956
40. Lune, *FROG 'Penguin'*, p. 174
41. Quoted in *ibid.*, p. 166
42. These figures are from NA. BT 31/45817. Board of Trade. Companies Registration Office. Company No 39827. Unique and Unity Cycle Company: *Ibid.*, Company No 314841. Pedigree Soft Toys Ltd.
43. MOC. Lines Brothers Archive. LINE 3/1/143. E. Gladwell to Mr Macfarlane, 3 February 1957
44. P. Hammond, *Tri-ang Railways: The Story of Rovex, Volume I, 1950–1965* (1993), p. 6
45. NA. BT 258/1382. Toy Manufacturers. Correspondence with Lines Brothers Ltd. Memorandum re planning application for Margate factory. n.d.
46. *Toy Trader and Exporter* (October 1956), p. 46
47. NA. BT 258/1382. Toy Manufacturers. Correspondence with Lines Brothers Ltd. Memo by J. C. Mather, 11 January 1962
48. *Ibid.* Office For Wales, Report June 1961
49. *Ibid.* Memo by L. H. Robinson, 4 May 1960. The figures refer to overseas sales achieved between February 1959 and January 1960
50. *Ibid.* Munich Consulate General to Board of Trade, 26 June 1958

51. *Ibid*. G. B. Harrison to Board of Trade, 1 August 1958
52. *Ibid*. Minute of meeting between J. L. May and J. J. Breslin, n.d.
53. Lines Brothers, *Annual Report* (1961), p. 14
54. Under this arrangement Hales became responsible for selling all of the Lines group's flying aeroplane kits, and for making independent arrangements for their production. IMA was thus left to concentrate solely on plastic kits and ready-to-fly models, releasing additional capacity for manufacturing Pedigree dolls and Ideal's toys.
55. Cited in *British Toys* (March 1962), p. 1
56. *The Observer*, 3 June 1962
57. BTMA. *Minute Book* (1962). Memorandum to Council, 13 June 1962. For a comment on his truculence see NA BT 258/1382. Toy Manufacturers. Correspondence with Lines Brothers Ltd. Memo by J. C. Mather, 11 January 1961
58. Lines Brothers, *Annual Report* (1961), p. 16
59. Because a standard accounting year was introduced across the entire group in 1960, the actual net profit figure reported was well over a million pounds as it covered eighteen months and two Christmas trading periods. The figure in this table represents the company's own calculation of a twelve-month equivalent.
60. NA. BT 258/1382. Toy Manufacturers. Correspondence with Lines Brothers Ltd. Memo by L. H. Robinson, 4 May 1960
61. *Ibid*. Memo by J. L. May, 18 February 1960
62. BTMA. *Minute Book* (1956–7). Council Meeting, 7 March 1957. He had adopted a similar attitude when he was still a member, requesting it on one occasion to warn any infringers of his patent for Wakouwa that legal action would be taken against them.
63. NA. BT 258/1382. Toy Manufacturers. Correspondence with Lines Brothers Ltd. W. Lines to Sir R. Powell, n.d.
64. In an interview with *The Times*, 22 December 1966

Chapter Five: The Wheels Come Off, 1961–1971

1. *The Times*, 24 July 1963
2. *Financial Times*, 2 February 1966

3. Walshe, 'Industrial organisation', p. 350
4. M. Gunter, *The Story of Wrenn: From Binns Road to Basildon* (2004), p. 6
5. *Economist*, 22 February 1964
6. *Daily Express*, 14 February 1964
7. MMM. Meccano Archives. B/ME/D/11. Lines' offer and letter to shareholders, 21 February 1964
8. *The Sun*, 5 October 1964
9. NA. BT 258/1383. Board of Trade: Industries and Manufactures Department. Toy Manufacturers: Correspondence with Lines Brothers Ltd. Report of the Deputy Consul General (Commercial) in New York, 4 December 1964
10. *Daily Express*, 14 February 1964
11. MOC. British toy-making project. Mr W. Graeme Lines (August 1913), p. 19
12. MMM. Meccano Archive. BME/28. Meccano Ltd., n.d. Typed note
13. *Ibid*. DME/21. Minute of meeting, 30 March 1965
14. Between 1964 and 1966, Meccano recorded net losses of £1,800,000. In 1967 there was a positive net profit – of £1,000. See Brown, *Factory of Dreams*, p. 151
15. This information is drawn from NA. BT 31/45829. Board of Trade: Companies Registration Office. File of dissolved companies. No of Company 31482. Pedigree Soft Toys Ltd.
16. Cited in Lines, *G & J to Tri-ang*, p. 225
17. NA. BT 258/1383. Board of Trade: Industries and Manufactures Department. Toy Manufacturers: Correspondence with Lines Brothers Ltd. Memo by L. H. Robinson, 4 May 1960
18. *The Times*, 7 December 1965
19. Lines Brothers, *Annual Report* (1966), p. 7
20. *The Times*, 20 November 1967
21. Lines Brothers, *Annual Report* (1967), p. 7
22. Author's interview with Richard Lines, 3 September 1993
23. *The Times*, 20 January 1968
24. BTMA. *Minute Book* (1967). Council Meeting, 14 December 1967
25. *The Times*, 14 November 1960
26. *Ibid.*, 22 December 1961

27. NA. BT 258/1383. Board of Trade: Industries and Manufactures Department. Toy Manufacturers: Correspondence with Lines Brothers Ltd. W. Lines to J. L. May, 6 November 1957. For his dismissal of the Japanese threat see *ibid.* Memo by L. H. Robinson, 4 May 1960
28. *Toy Trader and Exporter* (September 1956), p. 10
29. Cited in *ibid.* (October 1956), p. 43
30. *Toys International* (May–June 1970), p. 9
31. MOC. British toy-making project. Mr W. Graeme Lines (August 2013), p. 39
32. See M. Adolph, *Growing Up with Subbuteo* (Cheltenham, 2006), pp. 50, 182
33. *Guardian Society*, 30 May 2001
34. *Toys International* (March–April 1970), p. 27
35. *Ibid.* (July–August 1969), p. 8
36. Author's interview with Richard Lines, 3 September 1990
37. *The Times*, 6 August 1969
38. MMM. B/ME/D/11. W. G. Lines to Meccano, 16 April 1969
39. *Ibid.* W. M. Lines to fellow directors, 21 May 1969
40. *Ibid.* J. Mullen to W. G. Lines, 4 June 1969
41. *Ibid.* W. G. Lines to J. Mullen, 5 August 1969
42. *Ibid.* W. G. Lines to J. Mullen, 20 November 1969
43. *Toy Trader and Exporter Weekly Newssheet*, 16 May 1952
44. *Financial Times*, 27 January 1970
45. *The Times*, 23 December 1967
46. *Financial Times*, 31 January 1970
47. *Toys International* (March–April 1970), p. 8
48. Author's interview with Graeme Lines, 10 April 1991
49. *Toys International* (March–April 1970), pp. 24–7
50. MOC. P. Lines Archive. Uncatalogued. Memo marked 'Private and Confidential'
51. *Toys International* (November–December 1970), p. 26
52. MOC. British toy-making project. Mr W. Graeme Lines (August 2013), p. 49
53. *Ibid.*, p 15
54. Author's interview with Graeme Lines, 10 April 1991

55. Author's interview with Richard Lines, 3 September 1990
56. *The Times*, 2 July 1970
57. *Ibid.*, 14 July 1970
58. *Ibid.*, 1 September 1970
59. Lines Brothers, *Annual Report* (1969), p. 1
60. Drawn from *ibid.*, and *The Times*, 1 September 1969
61. MOC. P. Lines Archive. Uncatalogued. Lines Brothers to stockholders, 11 September 1970
62. *British Toys* (December 1970), p. 1
63. MOC. P. Lines Archive. Uncatalogued. Hamley Brothers Ltd. Typescript of statement by the chairman at the AGM 30 June 1971. *Ibid.*, Minutes of Hamley Brothers Board Meeting, 6 September 1971
64. The call and its contents were reported to the board a few days later. *Ibid.*, 8 September 1971
65. Author's interview with Graeme Lines, 10 April 1991
66. MOC. P. Lines Archive. Uncatalogued. Minutes of Hamley Brothers Board Meeting, 6 September 1971
67. *Ibid.* P. Lines to R. W. Munro, n.d.

Chapter Six: In the Breaker's Yard

1. *Games and Toys* (October 1971), p. 24
2. MOC. P. Lines Archive. Uncatalogued. Roger and Jane (indecipherable) to P. Lines, 8 September 1971. My italics.
3. See the comments made at the 54th AGM of the Trade Indemnity Co Ltd. as reported in *The Times*, 25 April 1972
4. *Ibid.*, 27 September 1971
5. *Ibid.*, 17 November 1971
6. See for instance, MOC. Peggy Lines Archive. Uncatalogued. R. Freeman to P. Lines, 2 July 1974
7. *British Toys* (December 1971), p. 1
8. *Sunday Times*, 11 June 1972
9. Author's interview with Graeme Lines, 10 April 1991
10. *The Times*, 24 November 1972. Years later he asserted in an interview that his reputation was undeserved, arguing that while he did recoup

some of his outlays by selling assets, the key to his success was a ruthless assault on costs. *Independent*, 26 February 1995
11. *British Toys* (December 1972), p. 6
12. MOC. British toy-making project. Mr W. Graeme Lines (August 2013), p. 41
13. *The Times*, 23 August 1971
14. *Toys International* (March–April 1972), p. 19
15. *Review of the UK Toy Industry* (1970), p. 76
16. Author's interview with J. G. Thomas, 29 August 1990
17. NA. LAB 35/566. Toy Manufacturing Wages Council. Minutes, 9 October 1947
18. *Sunday Times*, 11 June 1972
19. NA. BT 258/1383. Toy Manufacturers. Correspondence with Lines Brothers Ltd. Memo by F. T. Jones, 28 May 1963. This is an account of a meeting with Lines' representatives about establishing new factories in development areas. A briefing note in the file also refers to Walter's earlier refusal to site a proposed new doll dress-making operation in either the north east or Scotland.
20. Author's interview with Richard Lines, 3 September 1990
21. A. D. Chandler, 'The Development of Modern Management Structure in the US and the UK', in L. Hannah ed., *Management Strategy and Business Development* (1976) pp. 23-5
22. G. P. Dyas and H. T. Thanheiser, *The Emerging European Enterprise* (1976). For a general survey of the historiography see A. Colli, *The History of Family Business 1850–2000* (Cambridge, 2003)
23. *Toys International* (September–October 1970), p. 7
24. On this see Wilson, *British Business*, pp. 176-8
25. *Toys International* (March–April 1970), p. 35
26. *Ibid.* (November–December 1970), pp. 26-29. This accords well with the view that British firms in general looked for executives with 'leadership' and 'clubability' rather than specific professional management skills. See T. R. Gourvish, 'British Business and the Transition to a Corporate Economy: Entrepreneurship and Management Structures', *Business History*, XXIX, no 4. (1987), pp. 18-45
27. *Ibid.* (March–April 1972), p. 19

28. *Financial Times*, 1 May 1971. They were so outraged that they all refused offers of redeployment within the group and opted instead for redundancy.
29. *Toys International* (September–October 1970), p. 7
30. See K. D. Brown, 'The Collapse of the British Toy Industry, 1979–1984', *Economic History Review*, 46 (1993), pp. 592–606
31. Quoted in *Toys International* (September–October 1972), p. 13

Bibliography

Archives

British Toy Makers Association, Minutes and Annual Reports
Merseyside Maritime Museum. Meccano Archives
Victoria and Albert Museum of Childhood. P. Lines Archive. Uncatalogued
Victoria and Albert Museum of Childhood. Lines Brothers Archives

National Archives

BT 31/22987	BT 64/1751	BT 258/1382	LAB 11/2407
BT 31/24817	BT 64/4039	BT 258/1383	LAB 35/366-7
BT 31/45829	BT 64/4797	HO 192/1524	LAB 35/566-7
BT 31/46497	BT 177/1131	LAB 2/482	LAB 35/566
BT 55/80/87	BT 177/1132	LAB 2/ 906	LAB 41/250
BT 55/80/ 88	BT 215/1291	LAB 11/1799	

Official Publications

British Parliamentary Papers
Great Exhibition of 1851. Reports of the juries and commissioners (1852)

Newspapers

Daily Express
Graphic
Morning Chronicle
The Observer
The Sun
The Financial Times
The Sunday Times
The Times

Periodicals

Athletic Sports, Games and Toys
British Toys
Toy and Fancy Goods Trader
Toyshop and Fancy Goods Journal

Economist
Fancy Goods and Toy Trades Journal
Games and Toys
Games, Toys and Amusements
Toys International
Toy Trader
Toy Trader and Exporter
Toy Trader and Exporter Weekly Newssheet

Interviews

Author's interview with J. G. Thomas, 29 August 1990
Author's interview with Richard Lines, 3 September 1990
Author's interviews with Graeme Lines, 10 April 1991, 24 June 2011
MOC. British toy-making project. Mr W. Graeme Lines (August 2013)

Select Bibliography (Place of publication is London unless otherwise stated)

G. P. Bevan, *British Manufacturing industries* (1876)
Kenneth D. Brown, *The British Toy Business: A History Since 1700* (1996)
Kenneth D. Brown, 'Family failure? Lines Brothers Ltd., deceased 1971', in J. Astrachan ed., *Family Business Casebook Annual* (Georgia, 2005)
Kenneth D. Brown, *Factory of Dreams: A History of Meccano Limited, 1901–1979* (Lancaster, 2007)
Kenneth D. Brown, *Tri-ang Toys: The Story of Lines Brothers* (2012)
W. H. Cremer, *The Toys of the Little Folk* (1873)
Maurice Gunter, *The Story of Wrenn: From Binns Road to Basildon* (2004)
Pat Hammond, *Tri-ang Railways: The Story of Rovex. I, 1950–1965* (1993)
Peggy Lines, *From G & J to Tri-ang: The Lines Family Toy Business The First 80 Years* (Privately published. St Albans, 2015)
Richard Lines, *Tri-ang Toys, 1937–1938* (1988)
Richard Lines and Leif Hellstrom, *FROG Model Aircraft, 1932–1976* (1989)
Walter Lines, *Looking Backwards and Looking Forwards* (1958)
Colette Mansell, *The History of Sindy – Britain's Top Teenage Doll, 1962–1994* (1995)
Jon Mountfort, *Scalextric* (2009)

Graham Thompson, *Spot-On Diecast Models by Tri-ang* (1983)
Peter Van Lune, *FROG 'Penguin' Plastic Scale Model kits 1936–1950* (Privately published. Vianen, 2017)
David Veart, *Hello Girls and Boys! A New Zealand Toy Story* (Auckland, 2014)
Rod Ward, *A Concise History of Lines Bros Tri-ang Toys* (2013)
G. G. Weiner, *Juvenile Automobiles: A Pictorial History of Children's Pedal and Powered Vehicles* (1996)

Index

Adolph, Peter, 124–5
Airfix, 95, 128, 143, 148, 153
Allen & Co., 13, 15
Arkitex, 126
Arrow games, 143
Association of Toy Manufacturers
    and Wholesalers, 26–7, 31,
    40–1
Austen, Jane, 2
Ayres, F.H., 7

Babcock, H.K., 134
Baguley, G.F.R., 71, 77, 116, 134
Barbie doll, 126–7
Barclay Toy Group, 143–4
Barrington-Smith, Ken, 66
Bartley, George, 1–4, 8, 10
Bassett-Lowke, 11, 23, 55
Bentley, John, 144, 147
Bing Brothers, 67
Borwick, Colonel, 28–9, 31
Braddon, Mary, 3
Britain, William, 19, 55
    toy soldiers, 7, 11, 23, 95
British Industries Fair, 50, 64,
    99–100
    and government, 23–5, 55
    See also Lines Brothers
        Ltd: advertising and
        publicity

British toy business, 48, 50
    banks reluctance to invest in,
        30, 69, 71
    collapse of, 152–3
    early development of, 2–8,
        10–12
    employment in, 4–7, 11–12,
        39–41
    exports, 17, 55, 91, 95
    imports, 2–4, 41, 52, 63,
        121–3
    in First World War, 23–6
    manufacturers: *See* specific
        company names
    raw material shortages, 78,
        88–90
    tariffs and controls, 3–4, 63–4,
        80, 84, 88–91, 93, 121
    toy retailers and dealers,
        2–3, 11
British Toy Manufacturers
    Association, 85, 90,
    100, 106

Campbell, George, 31, 59
Cathcart, Alan, 97, 117
Chad Valley Company, 11, 23, 40,
    57, 126, 143
Chaplin, Charlie, 12
Childhood, 10, 94–5, 131, 145

Chiltern Toys, 11, 32, 86
Collinson Brothers, 7
Cremer, W.H., 7–8, 14
Crescent Toys, 86

Darby, J.O., 135–6, 138
Dickens, Charles, 5, 7
Dinky toys, 68, 95, 101, 115, 130, 145
Donne, David., 137, 139–40
Dullam, R.W., 58, 60
Dunbee Combex Marx, 153
    buys Rovex-Tri-ang, 143, 146
    offers to buy Lines Brothers, 139–40, 145

Edgeworth, Maria, 3

Farnell toy company, 11, 23
Freeman, Ralph, 30–1
FROG model aircraft, 69–70, 72–3, 96–8
    See also International Model Aircraft

Gallaher Ltd., 138, 145
Gamage, A.W., 21, 30
    department store, 13–14, 16, 60
Garner, Robert, 31
Gass, Marvin, 131
General Foods, 139, 145
German toy industry, 6, 17, 84
    British imports from, 2, 11, 25, 41
Great Exhibition, 6–7

Hamley's toy shop, 2, 57, 68, 70, 114
    becomes Hamleys of Regent Street, 143
    loans to Lines Brothers, 138, 140
    See also Lines Brothers Ltd: British acquisitions and subsidiaries
Harbutt, William, 11
Harrods department store, 13, 21, 34
Hollingshead, John, 9
Hornby, Frank, 11, 19, 39, 56
Hornby trains, 95, 98–9, 101, 113–15
Hot Wheels, 132, 146

Inglis, George, 59, 74, 77, 109, 117, 134
International Model Aircraft, 68–9, 79–80, 96–8
    See also Lines Brothers Ltd: British acquisitions and subsidiaries

Japanese toys, 25, 84, 121–2
Jones, George, 117

Kellner, George, boats, 66

Lego, 121, 126–7
Lesney Matchbox, 101, 126, 128, 132, 146, 153
Levi, Leone, 5
Lines, Arthur, 53, 76, 91, 109, 153
    as director of Lines Brothers Ltd., 31, 71–3, 89, 107, 110

as director of Lines Brothers
  subsidiaries, 51, 59, 77, 116
at G. & J. Lines, 18–19
management role and style, 33,
  47, 52, 74
war service, 24, 29
Lines Brothers Ltd:
  advertising and publicity, 35,
    38–9, 46, 123, 127–8, 130–1,
    133
    British Industries Fair, 23, 39,
      66–7, 75
    catalogues, 33–4, 52, 64, 85
    London showrooms, 45,
      73, 114
    toy fair, 99–101, 130
    trade marks, 33, 51, 149
    Tri-ang Magazine, 114
  British acquisitions and
    subsidiaries:
    A. A. Hales, 105, 113, 143
    Arrow Games, 143
    Hamley Brothers, 58–60, 73,
      99, 116–17, 140
    International Model Aircraft,
      69–70, 72–3, 85, 116–17, 148
    Lipkin, Ralph, 105, 119
    Meccano Ltd., 110, 113–16,
      129, 132–3, 146–8
    Minic Ltd., 97
    Minimodels Ltd., 102,
      129–30, 134, 137
    Pearce, W. & Co., 89, 116
    Pedigree, 73, 77, 85, 97, 116,
      129, 143, 148
    Rovex, 98, 105, 110, 129–30
    Shuresta, 113, 129, 137, 151
    Simpson, Fawcett & Co., 99
    Subbuteo Ltd., 113, 125
    Unique and Unity Cycle
      Company, 51, 85, 95, 97,
      116–17, 143
    Walker Industries, 113
    Wrenn, G. & R., 113, 148
    Young and Fogg, 97
    Youngsters, 99, 129, 143
    See also individual company
      names
  finance:
    capitalisation, 31, 36, 46,
      71, 75–6, 88, 93, 104,
      118–19
    dividends, 78, 82, 85, 106, 111,
      118–19, 136
  organisation and structure, 73,
    85, 150–2
    Articles of Association, 31, 71
    becomes public company,
      70–1
    board membership, 31, 71,
      134–5
    collapse, 135–41, 146–53
    dissolution, 142–4
    divisional organisation
      117–18, 133
    establishment, 28–31
    example of personal
      capitalism, 52, 70, 73, 116
    research department, 124
    royal warrant, 58

overseas:
  Argentina, 61–2
  Australia, 93, 99, 103, 113, 142
  Canada, 92, 103, 110–11, 116, 118, 142, 149
  France, 104, 110–11, 114, 118, 147, 149
  Germany, 104, 111
  New Zealand, 92, 103, 116–17
  South Africa, 34, 37, 93–4, 103, 113, 143
  USA, 55, 92, 104–105, 110–11, 115
premises:
  Belfast, 87–8, 101, 119, 137, 148–9
  Canterbury, 97, 119
  Hatcham Works, 29, 31–2, 45, 51
  Margate, 99, 119, 122
  Merthyr, 86–7, 99, 102, 109 148–9
  Merton, 45–7, 58, 77, 85–6, 95, 99, 109, 119, 144
  Oldham, 50–1
  Richmond, 98
products, 64, 95, 97–8, 119, 124–5, 137, 145–6
  baby carriages and prams, 35–6, 37, 43, 48–9, 64, 81, 102, 128
  board games, 126
  boats, 65, 73, 96
  cycles and scooters, 35, 44, 95, 103, 125
  dolls, 73, 129–130
  dolls' house furniture, 38, 41, 43
  dolls' houses, 34, 37, 43, 49, 66, 69
  dolls' prams, 34, 37, 43, 49, 67
  educational toys, 65
  licensing deals, 104–105, 112
  mechanical toys, 67–8
  nursery furniture, 64–5
  packaging, 37–8, 49, 96, 115
  pedal cars, 33–4, 37, 44, 49, 61, 67, 96
  prices, 35, 37, 43, 48, 61, 67, 78, 93
  steel toys, 49, 66–7
  rocking horses, 33, 35, 66
  swimming pools, 112–13
  wooden toys, 33, 37, 43–4, 49, 66, 95, 144
  See also Arkitex, FROG aircraft, Meccano sets, Minic, Pedigree dolls, Pedigree prams, Pedigree soft toys, Penguin range, Puff-Puff engines, Scalextric, Sindy doll, Spot-On diecast, Tri-ang trains
turnover and profitability:
  exports, 34–5, 51–2, 80, 91–2, 95, 102–103
  in Second World War, 82
  interwar, 36, 43, 47–8, 51, 55–60, 64

Index 181

post 1945, 93, 105–106, 110–11, 118–20, 128–38
workforce, 51
   industrial relations, 35, 147
   pay and conditions, 32–3, 47
   productivity, 48, 133, 147–8
   size, 40, 45, 47, 73, 81, 95, 102, 137
Lines, George (born 1841), 8, 12, 18
Lines, George (born 1888), 18, 29, 43, 84, 107, 116
   at Lines Brothers, 57, 75
Lines, G. & J., 8, 24–6, 45, 48
   becomes limited company, 18
   catalogues, 14, 19, 24
   employees, 12–13, 22–3, 32
   exports, 17–18
   factories, 12, 20–3
   failure, 56–7
   products, 12, 16
      baby carriages, 13, 16
      cycles and scooters, 15, 24
      dolls' houses, 15–16
      dolls' prams, 15, 20
      pedal cars, 15, 19–20, 24, 34
      rocking horses, 12–14, 23–4
      wooden toys, 12, 14, 16, 24
   trade mark, 19
   turnover, 17, 26
Lines, Graeme, 55, 130–1, 139, 144
   as managing director of Meccano Ltd., 115–16, 129–30, 148
   career, 109–10, 151
   critical of Lines Brothers, 123–4, 134, 150
   resignation, 134–5
   response to Mattel Inc., 132–3
Lines, John, 110, 135
Lines, Joseph, 8, 12
   conservatism, 20, 22, 24, 26–7, 39
   death, 57
   relations with brother, 18
   relations with sons, 20–22, 29, 56–7
Lines, Mary, 18, 21, 30, 59
Lines, Moray, 102–103, 116, 139
   as chairman and managing director of Lines Brothers Ltd., 121, 129, 132, 137, 152
   career, 109–10
   comments on company performance, 110–11, 118–20, 128, 135–6
   opinions, 114, 120, 127
   resignation 135–6, 138
Lines, Peggy, 72
   archive, 34, 62
   as chair of Hamleys, 109, 140, 143
Lines, Peter, 110, 151
Lines, Richard:
   career, 110, 117, 151
   opinions, 96, 120, 128, 134–5, 149
   resignation, 135
Lines, Walter, 17, 26, 28, 136, 153
   career:
      as director of Lines Brothers Ltd., 31, 36, 71, 113, 124, 135–6, 151

as director of Lines Brothers
subsidiaries, 51, 58, 77, 116
Association of Toy
Manufacturers and
Wholesalers, 31, 42, 53, 63
at G. & J. Lines, 13, 15–16,
18–19, 34, 58
BIF Advisory Committee, 53
British Toy Manufacturers
Association, 85, 100
London and South East
Regional Board for
Industry, 87
Ramsden Committee, 87
Regent Street Association, 60
retirement, 102, 105, 109
Toy Trade Board, 53, 147
character:
attention to detail, 34, 52, 60,
75, 146
attitude to employees, 74–5,
116, 147
autocratic, 71, 105, 107, 109,
122, 134
energy, 58, 107
impatience with bureaucracy,
79–81, 85, 86–8, 91, 94
management style, 74–5, 105,
109, 117
optimism, 56–7, 64
passion for toy making, 18, 33,
35, 44, 75, 105, 144
self-importance, 53,
81, 107–108
views on tariffs, 41–2, 52, 62–3

personal:
death, 144
engagement, 43
income and wealth, 53, 76,
110, 145
war service, 24, 29
Lines, Will, 29–30, 36, 53, 109, 153
as director of Lines Brothers
Ltd., 31–2, 71, 76, 107, 116
as director of Lines Brothers
subsidiaries, 51, 59, 77, 116
at G. & J. Lines, 12, 15, 18–20, 24
death, 109
disaffection with his father, 27–8
management style and role, 33,
65, 74, 116
Lines, Winifred, 59
Lucas, Gerald, 133–4, 151

Manchester toy fair, 50–1, 55,
64, 100
Mansour, Joe, 69–70, 72, 96–7
Marx, Louis, 84, 86, 122, 139
Mattel Inc., 123, 126–7, 132, 150
Mayhew, Henry, 4–6
McCulloch, J.R., 3
Meccano Ltd., 23, 45, 50, 55–6, 68,
143, 153
See also Lines Brothers: Ltd:
British acquisitions and
subsidiaries
See also Lines, Graeme
Meccano sets, 11, 95, 115, 126, 145
Merrythought Ltd., 77, 95
Mettoy, 86, 101, 128, 153

Minic, 68, 73, 96–7, 99, 102
Minimodels Ltd., 101–102
    See also Lines Brothers Ltd:
        British acquisitions and
        subsidiaries
Munn, James, 51
Munro, R.C., 31, 134

Nicolson, David, 134, 139–40

Ormside Street, See Lines Brothers
    Ltd: premises: Hatcham
    Works
Osler, Thomas, 1

Pearce W. & Co, See Lines Brothers
    Ltd: British acquisitions
    and subsidiaries
Pedigree
    Soft Toy Company, 79, 110
        See also Lines Brothers Ltd:
            British acquisitions and
            subsidiaries
    dolls, 77, 98–9, 105, 126–7
    prams, 43, 52
    soft toys, 77, 89
PE Management Consultants,
    133–4
Penguin range, 72, 80, 96–8
Puff-Puff engines, 44

Rae, James, 53, 69–70, 81
Raleigh Industries, 125, 128, 142, 144
Reeves, Maud Pember, 9
Retail price maintenance, 120

Ridingbery, J. E., 7
Roberts Brothers, 11, 23, 40
Rowntree, Seebohm, 9

Safeguarding of Industries Act
    inquiry, 40–1
Scalextric, 101–102, 113–14, 125–6,
    130, 145
Sindy doll, 126–7, 145
Spot-On diecast, 101, 114–15, 126
Subbuteo, 125

Thrower, Peter, 137, 139,
    142, 152
Toy and Fancy Goods Trade
    Federation, 42
Toys:
    definitions, 3
    dolls, 1–3, 6–7
    dolls' houses, 7
    educational, 3, 10
    market for, 1–3, 8–10, 83–5,
        94–5, 124, 145
    rocking horses, 3, 5, 7
    wooden, 6, 48
        See also Lines Brothers Ltd:
            products
        See also Lines, G. & J:
            products
Toy Trade Board, 32, 40
Tri-ang trains, 98–9, 110,
    113–14, 126

Unique and Unity Cycle Co.,
    35, 125

See also Lines Brothers Ltd:
    British acquisitions and
      subsidiaries
Upsdell, Robert, 143–4, 147, 151
US toy industry, 25, 55, 84, 122–3
    See also Marx, Louis
    See also Mattel Inc.

Waddingtons Ltd., 125–6
Williams, E.E., 11
Wilmot, Charles, 68–70, 72, 96–7
Wilmot, John, 68–9